T0108390

Praise for *Build Bridges, Not Walls*

"As more and more millions are forced to migrate to survive, and as militarized borders disfigure an ever-increasing portion of the Earth's surface, Todd Miller's analysis and reporting have become essential to understanding both the world in which we live and the one for which we have to fight. In *Build Bridges, Not Walls*, Miller writes with poetry, unfailing critical intelligence, and most of all with heart. He cuts through the facile media myths and escapes the paralyzing constraints of a political 'debate' that functions mainly to obscure the unconscionable inequalities that borders everywhere secure. In its soulfulness, its profound moral imagination, and its vision of radical solidarity, Todd Miller's work is as indispensable as the love that so palpably guides it."

—Ben Ehrenreich, author of *Desert Notebooks:
A Road Map for the End of Time*

"Todd Miller lays bare the senselessness and soullessness of the nation-state and its borders and border walls, and reimagines, in their place, a complete and total restoration, therefore redemption, of who we are, and of who we are in desperate need of becoming."

—Brandon Shimoda, author of *The Grave on the Wall*

"All of Todd Miller's work is essential reading, but *Build Bridges, Not Walls* is his most compelling, insightful book yet. Miller's storytelling is woven together with his rigorous research on the inner workings of border control systems and how they worsen the concentration of global wealth and the suffering caused by climate change. *Build Bridges, Not Walls* makes a convincing argument for border abolition that builds on the police and prison abolition movement's insights, helping us see that the plans to make border enforcement more fair are shams, and that imagining and creating a world without borders is entirely possible."

—Dean Spade, author of *Mutual Aid:
Building Solidarity During This Crisis (and the Next)*

"Based on years of work as a journalist and his engagements with migrants, Miller calls us to see how borders subject millions of people to violence, dehumanization, and early death. More important, he highlights the urgent necessity to abolish not only borders, but the nation-state itself. Drawing on the work of abolitionist movement leaders, this book points toward the radical opening of the imagination urgently needed to transform walls into bridges."

—A. Naomi Paik, author of *Bans, Walls, Raids, Sanctuary:
Understanding U.S. Immigration for the Twenty-First Century*

"Todd Miller and his four-year-old son William invite us to imagine future bicycles and playgrounds where we now see the steel bollards of border walls. Drawing on years of reporting and the work of scholars, thinkers, and activists from around the world—such as Bayo Akomolafe's concepts of 'fugitive spirit' and 'modest criminality'—Miller builds a case for imagining the seemingly impractical, the supposedly impossible idea of a living in a world without borders, and without the states that so desperately, and so violently, cling to them."

—John Gibler, author of *Torn from the World: A Guerrilla's Escape from a Secret Prison in Mexico*

"By documenting the human toll of border walls, expanded security, and racialized policing, Miller makes the urgent case to abolish borders now."

—Reece Jones, author of *White Borders*

"Todd Miller's *Build Bridges, Not Walls* is an eloquent and urgent call to dismantle the narrative of 'border security,' denouncing this sinister concept not as a policy seeking to protect the general population, but rather 'as an apparatus to enforce extreme inequalities and power imbalances.' Through careful reporting and vivid personal experience, Miller illuminates the immediate need to bring people closer in an era of dehumanizing violence that is at the heart of U.S. political discourse and institutions."

—Oswaldo Zavala, journalist and professor of Latin American literature and culture at the City University of New York and author of *Drug Cartels Do Not Exist: Narcotrafficking and Culture in Mexico*

"Todd Miller's deeply reported, empathetic writing on the American border is some of the most essential journalism being done in America today. It's impossible to read his work without coming away changed."

—Adam Conover, creator and host of *Adam Ruins Everything*

Praise for *Storming The Wall: Climate Change, Migration, and Homeland Security*

RECIPIENT OF THE 2018 IZZY AWARD FOR EXCELLENCE IN INVESTIGATIVE JOURNALISM

"Every so often a book comes along that can dramatically change, or elevate, one's thinking about a global problem. Much like Naomi Klein's books, Todd Miller's *Storming the Wall* is such a book and deserves far more attention and discussion."

—Izzy Award Judges, Ithaca College

"A galvanizing forecast of global warming's endgame and a powerful indictment of America's current stance."

—*Kirkus Reviews*

"Nothing will test human institutions like climate change in this century—as this book makes crystal clear, people on the move from rising waters, spreading deserts, and endless storms could profoundly destabilize our civilizations unless we seize the chance to reimagine our relationships to each other. This is no drill, but it is a test, and it will be graded pass-fail."

—Bill McKibben, author of *Eaarth: Making a Life on a Tough New Planet*

BUILD BRIDGES, NOT WALLS

Open Media Series Editor: Greg Ruggiero

Cover design by Victor Mingovits

ISBN: 978-0-87286-834-2

Library of Congress Cataloging-in-Publication Data

Names: Miller, Todd, 1970– author.
Title: Build bridges, not walls / by Todd Miller.
Description: San Francisco : City Lights Books, 2021. |
Series: Open media series
Identifiers: LCCN 2020040807 (print) | LCCN 2020040808 (ebook) | ISBN
9780872868342 (paperback) | ISBN 9780872868366 (epub)
Subjects: LCSH: United States—Emigration and immigration—Government
policy. | Mexico—Emigration and immigration. | Central
America—Emigration and immigration. | Illegal aliens—United States—Social
conditions. | Immigrants—United States—Social conditions. | Mexican-American
Border Region—Social conditions.
Classification: LCC JV6483 .M559 2021 (print) | LCC JV6483 (ebook) | DDC
325.73—dc23
LC record available at https://lccn.loc.gov/2020040807
LC ebook record available at https://lccn.loc.gov/2020040808

City Lights Books are published at the City Lights Bookstore
261 Columbus Avenue, San Francisco, CA 94133
www.citylights.com

BUILD BRIDGES, NOT WALLS

A Journey to a World Without Borders

TODD MILLER

CITY LIGHTS BOOKS | Open Media Series

SAN FRANCISCO

For Sofia and William, and the future generations you represent.

ILLUSTRATIONS

CONTENTS

Sube a nacer conmigo, hermano.

—Pablo Neruda, "Canto XII"

BUILD BRIDGES, NOT WALLS

ONE

FROM THE
BROKEN PIECES

The hand between the candle and the wall
Grows large on the wall...
It must be that the hand
Has a will to grow larger on the wall,
To grow larger and heavier and stronger than
The wall...

—Wallace Stevens, from "Poem with Rhythms"

WE ARE ALL AT THE BORDER NOW

I SEE A man on the edge of the road. He looks both desperate and ragged and waves his arms for me to pull over my car. We are in southern Arizona, about twenty miles north of the U.S.-Mexico border. Behind the man is the Sonoran Desert—beautiful twisting saguaros, prickly pear, and cholla cacti—the living earth historically inhabited by the indigenous communities of the Tohono O'odham Nation. As I stop, the man rushes to my side of the car. Speaking in Spanish, he tells me his name is Juan Carlos. He tells me he is from Guatemala. He gulps down the water I offer him and asks if I can give him a ride to the nearest town.

Just an hour earlier, majestic saguaros and elegant ocotillos surrounded me as I hiked out of the Baboquivari Peak Wilderness with Tohono O'odham elder David Garcia. The night before, we had seen two heavily armed U.S. Border Patrol agents monitoring a trail we used to reach the peak of the mountain.

The Baboquivari Peak, where Garcia once fasted for many days to ask for guidance, is sacred to the Tohono O'odham. At points along the path up the slope, we could see layers of mountains extending for hundreds of miles, deep into Mexico. When you are up there you do not see the Border Patrol. You do not see the fleet of green-striped ground vehicles. You do not see the border wall. From up there, the border does not exist. Nations do not exist. The Earth appears as one uninterrupted landscape. Absorbing such a view can alter one's feelings and consciousness in a way few things can.

Edgar Mitchell was the sixth person to set foot on the moon. He described seeing the large, glowing globe of planet Earth as deeply moving: "It was a beautiful, harmonious, peaceful-looking planet, blue with white clouds, and one that gave you a deep sense...of home, of being, of identity. It is what I prefer to call instant global consciousness." Seeing the land without political boundaries became an insight into what connects us to one another and the planet as a whole. The revelation was sincere and direct. High in the Tohono O'odham's sacred territory, I felt something similar to what Mitchell describes.

Parked on the side of the road, Juan Carlos asking me for the ride, awareness of our fractured world comes crashing back. I can't see the agents, surveillance cameras, and sensors, but I know they are all around. I can feel them. Above, one of many drones in the U.S. arsenal could be documenting the moment and streaming data about our location and movements. Agents are armed not only with weapons and technology, but with laws. One such law forbids me from giving Juan Carlos a ride. Doing so would further his unauthorized presence in the United States. If caught, I could be nailed with a federal crime, a felony. In essence, I could get prison time for showing kindness to a stranger.

But wouldn't it be a crime to leave somebody there, knowing that doing so could lead to their death? And wouldn't refusing to help a person in distress due to their ethnicity be racism of the most blatant kind? This sort of racism is encoded into the very concept of "border security" and its regime of agents, technologies, policies, bureaucracies, and violent vigilantes. With no sign of any nearby town, I am forced to contemplate Juan's skin complexion, his disheveled clothes, and his Spanish-only speech. As one official from the Department of Homeland Security told the *New York Times*, "We can't do our job without taking ethnicity into account. We are very dependent on that."

This is happening in the Arizona desert, but I could have been talking with someone skirting a checkpoint in southern Mexico, or with a person crossing the Mona Strait from the Dominican shores to Puerto Rico in a rickety boat, or with people crammed in a cargo ship going from Libya to Italy or Turkey to Greece. This could've been a person crossing from Syria to Jordan, from Somalia to Kenya, from Bangladesh to India, or from the Occupied Palestinian Territories into Israel. There are more people on the move, and crossing borders, than ever before. Approximately 258 million people are currently living outside the country of their birth, a sure undercount given the difficulty of counting undocumented people.

A similar scene could unfold *within* countries too, since immigration enforcement is hardly limited to national perimeters. In the United States, border enforcement could take place on an Amtrak train in Rochester, Buffalo, Erie, or Detroit, where armed agents board trains and ask people for their papers. We could have been in any of countless U.S. cities where Immigration and Customs Enforcement agents operate twenty-four hours a day hunting for people who are here without authorization. In Mexico, immigration agents regularly board buses throughout the country. For example, I once saw a man pulled off a bus after he said he lived in San Cristóbal de los Angeles instead of San Cristóbal de las Casas. On another occasion, when I was on a bus in the Dominican Republic near the border with Haiti, an immigration agent asked every black passenger for their papers, but ignored me even as I sat there attentively with passport in hand. And then, in contrast, at the edge of a Somali neighborhood in Nairobi I was stopped and interrogated for half an hour as the immigration agent sifted through my papers.

Now I am in the U.S. borderlands with Juan Carlos, and forced to make a decision. In this book, I reflect on why I hesitate when Juan Carlos asks me for a ride. And as I search for an answer, I find that there is a much bigger problem to tackle: Why am I forced to make such a decision in the first place? Why am I compelled to be complicit either with enforcing authoritarian law or with upholding our common humanity, with building a wall or building a bridge?

What follows is a journey through more than twenty-five years living and working as a journalist, writer, educator, and perennial student of and in the world's borderlands. In the process I have met many people who influenced my thinking profoundly—and you will meet some of them here—Tojolabal Zapatistas in southern Mexico, a Franciscan friar in the Arizona borderlands, a border crosser escaping the ravages of climate change, an open-hearted Border Patrol agent, and modern-day abolitionists, among many other provocative thinkers and doers in this world who dare defy conventional thought and boundaries.

In *Build Bridges, Not Walls* I look at the ways that divisions have been imposed, permitted, and accepted over decades, regardless of who is the U.S. president. But I also examine the natural inclination of human beings to be empathic with one another, to forge solidarities with each other, and how such inclinations contrast with the borders that invoke and perpetuate chronic forms of racial and economic injustice. I welcome you to the journey on these pages. Here you will find a call for abolitionist resistance through kindness—a fugitive kindness that has edge, that shatters unjust laws and is based in solidarity. And here you will find an aspiration to create something beautiful, something human, from the broken pieces.

SANCTUARY

ON A COLD evening in January 2018, the very same night of Donald Trump's first State of the Union Address, several students and I visited the San Juan Bosco shelter in Nogales, Mexico. In the shelter's chapel was a group of people, many recently expelled from the United States, seated in metal chairs. The funeral of a six-week-old baby from Honduras a few days before had left a somber mood that still weighed heavily in the space. The child had died of exposure to the cold. The baby's young, moneyless parents had just reached Nogales en route to the United States when the tragic death occurred.

After the students and I introduced ourselves, an older woman immediately asked: "Why are you here?" She paused. She had a blanket around her shoulders like a shawl, to fend off the cold evening air. "What benefit does it bring us?"

A long and uncomfortable pause followed, partly while I interpreted her question from Spanish to English, and partly because we had no immediate answer. Why were we there? Was it because we were simply a class, learning about border issues for a grade? Or was it something else all of us wished to be part of, was it that we wanted to learn how to topple the border barrier between us? Whatever it was, the woman seemed to carry a wisdom beyond us, leaving us speechless. A chair scratched against the floor, and a person in the back coughed. As the uncomfortable pause persisted, I realized that I, too, was baffled. The political and economic conditions appeared to be so entrenched that change did seem virtually impossible. Trump was about to roll out his plans on live television. He was about to make the claim that "open borders" were allowing "drugs and gangs to pour into our most vulnerable communities," and to claim that "millions of low-wage workers" would "compete for jobs and wages against the poorest Americans." Trump may have even said this at the precise moment the woman asked her question, as we stood there looking at each other, hoping that somebody in the group might answer.

The thing was, at that moment there was no practical alternative to the long legacy of border militarization to even talk about. Opposition to the wall among Democrats seemed to gain prominence only after the 2016 election. But what they offered were simply different forms of the same "wall," such as so-called "smart walls," technology meant to monitor, sort, and exclude people with even greater efficiency than a standard barrier. Just a week before, Representative Henry Cuellar had penned an op-ed for CNN titled "The answer to border security is technology, not wall." The Texas Democrat characterized the wall as a fourteenth-century solution to a twenty-first-century challenge. "Instead of a wall," Cuellar wrote, "we should increase the use of modern technology, including cameras, fixed towers and aerial and underground sensors." This position has become a standard one for the Democratic Party and was reflected in the Joe Biden administration's immigration platform when he took office in 2021. Unmentioned in Cuellar's op-ed was that some of the top border contractors—companies such as Northrop Grumman, Caterpillar, Boeing, and Lockheed Martin—were lining his coffers to support his 2018 reelection campaign. And two of the top prison management companies contracted by Immigration and Customs Enforcement—GEO Group and CoreCivic—contributed a whopping $55 million to his war chest.

I suppose we could have repeated the cliché that the "immigration system is broken" and we have to fix it. But what if it really was functioning entirely as designed? We could have told her that we would push for reform. But what exactly is meant by the phrase "comprehensive immigration reform"? It is true that new laws might contain provisions for a better legalization process and a more permanent status for beneficiaries of Deferred Action on Childhood Arrival (DACA) who fit a certain set of criteria. But that would in no way help the people sitting before us on that cold night in Nogales. In fact, if the history of comprehensive immigration reform were any indication, any new policy would likely involve even more guns, guards, and gates. The 2013 bipartisan "gang of eight" reform bill—the last one passed by the U.S. Senate but rejected in the House—had $45 billion going to the border over a ten-year period. The budget's intention was to double the forces of the Border Patrol and triple the capacity of its "zero tolerance" Operation Streamline, which incarcerates border-crossers by the tens of thousands each year. Hungry to tap the bulging purse, corporations lobbied for loads of border technology to be purchased as part of the reform. Three companies—Northrop Grumman, United Technologies, and EADS North America—pumped more than $70,000 per day into their lobbying efforts. This meant more VADER systems (man-hunting radar manufactured by Northrop Grumman), more Blackhawk helicopters (fifteen of them from United Technologies, a company then about to be bought by Lockheed Martin), and eight helicopters from EADS North America.

That is the long-term vision planned for the people in the shelter, and neither we nor they are invited to the planning sessions. It doesn't matter if you are on the move because droughts wilted your crops, hurricanes blasted your house, mines poisoned your water, or floods swallowed your land, or you are fleeing murderous persecution and extortion, or violent economic dispossession by corporate or local oligarchies. It doesn't matter if you are skipping meals for your children, or if you are fleeing for your very life.

I have gone to conferences and conventions involving companies and government in Phoenix, Paris, Tel Aviv, Mexico City, San Antonio, El Paso, and Washington, D.C., to observe how the long-term vision is monetized and dehumanized. There are lots of carpeted convention centers filled with vendors hungry to sell robots, drones, surveillance cameras, radar systems, license plate scanners, facial recognition systems, iris recognition software, guns, sunglasses, ready-to-eat meals, and insta-latrines. I remember one man selling a portable, easy-to-deploy metal barrier capable of stopping a truck at high speeds. The material it was made of was on display at the expo.

When I asked the salesman if the stuff could really stop a Mack Truck, as his sales video indicated, his response was, "You better believe it. This is evolution. This is the future." When I saw him again later that day, he called me over with semi-anxious eyes and asked me where he could find buyers for his product. Startled that he was asking me, I could only point to my name tag indicating that I was a journalist.

A few hours later, I was in front of a Raytheon salesman who was hawking the latest technology for acoustic detection that, and

11

I couldn't get this out of my mind, looked like the sad, maligned Christmas tree from *Charlie Brown*.

"It's to detect where bullets are shot from," he told me.

"Bullets are flying over the border?" I asked, knowing the answer to my own question.

"You'd be surprised," he told me, "not every day, but every other day." He left it to the world of long-cultivated assumptions as to who was doing the shooting.

While pointing to his product—a desert-colored pole with microphones extending from its top in all directions—he said that it could be mounted on the border wall "every quarter mile or so." The vision was tangible and precise, the raw imagination of the constantly churning border-industrial complex. Within constraints, it is constantly imagining how to monetize a future world of increasingly militarized compliance, caste, exclusion, and hierarchy, with next to no pushback or dissent.

Most of us are not involved in debating the future marketed at these sales conventions, we're not at the closed-door meetings, the hotel rooms, the golf courses where future borderscapes are mapped out, and where money begins to line the pockets of influential policy-makers. This is especially true of the people sitting at the shelter, the people who are targets of the acoustic detection systems, Mack Truck–stopping walls, and infrared goggles. For forty years, border and immigration enforcement budgets have gone up, year after year, with little or no public consultation or debate.

It has been amazing to me, as I've traveled the country for the past decade or so speaking on these topics, to see the general lack of awareness about how much these border and immigration enforcement budgets have increased over the last four decades. At the advent of the Ronald Reagan presidency in 1980, the annual border and immigration budget was $349 million, through the Immigration and Naturalization Service, (INS). In 2020, the combined budget of its superseding agencies, Customs and Border Protection (CBP) and Immigration and Customs Enforcement (ICE), exceeded $25 billion. That is a 6,000 percent increase.

These increases are fueled by rhetoric that uses the seemingly incontestable term "security," with no debate at all. But when I began to examine the appropriations process—the one through which budgets like that of the Department of Homeland Security (DHS) are determined, including how much money is earmarked for certain contracts and certain companies—I found the level of public ignorance less startling. In fact, the debate about the future happens every year; it's just that most of us are not invited. Big corporations such as Northrop Grumman, Elbit Systems, General Atomics, and Deloitte show up in throngs, but behind closed doors that keep you and me out.

The absence of public involvement was on full display in 2006 when Michael Jackson, an official with CBP, stood before private industry representatives. When discussing the new technology program on the border, known as SBInet, he said: "This is an unusual invitation. I want to make sure you have it clearly, that we're asking you to come back and tell us how to do our business. We're asking you. We're inviting you to tell us how to run our organization." As a former executive with Lockheed Martin, Jackson knew how corporations and the U.S. government interact, free from public oversight. And after Jackson made that comment, from 2006 to 2018, CBP and ICE doled out 99,000 contracts worth approximately $45 billion, equivalent to the accumulated border and immigration enforcement budgets from 1975 to 2002. That's twenty-seven years of budgets *combined*.

The U.S. government and multinational corporations project enforcement scenarios decades into the future, imagining a world increasingly destabilized due to mass migrations caused by catastrophic climate change. Countries such as the United States and Australia need to envision erecting "defensive fortresses" in response, according to a 2003 Pentagon report. In March 2013, Admiral Samuel J. Locklear III, the commander of the United States Pacific Command, said that global warming was the greatest threat the United States faced. Mass destabilization, he said, "is probably the most likely thing that is going to happen [to] cripple the security environment, probably more likely than the other scenarios we all often talk about."

Today, as the scientific basis for catastrophic climate change has become hard to avoid even for its most fervent deniers, officials are explicitly placing weather and environmental events in the same threat landscape as terrorism or organized crime. As Admiral Craig Faller, commander of Southern Command, said during a July

2020 hearing titled National Security Challenges and U.S. Military Activity in North and South America, "The ability to rapidly respond to events, whether it's a weather event, or an environmental event, a terrorist attack, [or a] transnational criminal organization, is important. So we continue to watch that closely and ensure that our exercise programs, our security cooperation programs, emphasize the partners' capacity to do that, because as we see in some of these massive hurricanes, no one nation has the ability to do that alone." The seemingly bland term "security cooperation programs" means that the United States is redefining its border, training border guards and sending armored patrol vehicles and guns and other resources not only to Central American and Caribbean countries, but also deep into South America, with CBP attachés now in Brasilia and Bogotá. As with the war on drugs and the war on terror, there is now a war on climate change, aimed not at mitigating carbon emissions in the biosphere, but at erecting "defensive fortresses" against the people most impacted, the people on the move. As author, scholar, and activist Harsha Walia writes, emphasizing the need to reframe the conversation around borders, there isn't a border crisis, there is a "displacement crisis."

Efforts to advance comprehensive immigration reform take place today against this background of increasingly dystopic security forecasts. Despite the fact that the U.S. Border Patrol and ICE remain sacrosanct, with ever more resources, a movement to abolish ICE emerged in 2018 and began to pry open this locked door. However, Democrats—as is often their way—voiced support and watered it down at the same time. For them, it became a call for reforms. Democrats have avoided taking on CBP in any substantial way (though representative Alexandria Ocasio-Cortez is a notable exception), because questioning territorial boundaries and their enforcement apparatus remains far beyond the party's parameters of acceptable debate. The debate is usually silenced by one phrase—"every country has the right to protect its borders"—and it's left for the crickets to guess who and what actually gets protected and how.

The difficulty of collaborating on long-term alternatives became apparent to me when the nonprofit Institute for the Future (IFTF) invited me to a workshop in 2019. The purpose of the workshop was to think systemically and imaginatively about the future of immigration. The IFTF invited experts from across the country, many people working on the front lines, and many who were undocumented and refugees themselves, to imagine different possible futures for immigration, from most desired to worst-case scenarios. One revelation that emerged at the beginning of the conference was that front-line workers weren't able to think at all about the future, let alone strategize. There was no time. The demand of dealing with constant emergencies in real time overwhelmed them.

At the 2018 State of the Union Address, President Trump said, "The United States is a compassionate nation. We are proud that we do more than any other country to help the needy, the struggling, the underprivileged all over the world. But as president of the United States, my loyalty, my greatest compassion, and my constant concern is for America's children." Surely not words the people in the Nogales shelter would find comforting.

Simultaneously, there was something liberating about standing on the other side of the U.S. border, in a space where there was little to no awareness that the State of the Union was even happening. For just a moment we were free from U.S. discourse and its claustrophobic parameters of what was considered debatable and what was not. In this sense, being there freed us from our own preconceptions, from the scrolling confines of smartphones, from headlines based on whatever view we were supposed to hold. As the pause continued, we could feel the cold Nogales night seeping through the cracks, but also something more glorious, a conversation that was going to challenge not only the walls enclosing the United States, but also the walls within ourselves. It was as if questions that are never asked publicly in the United States were suddenly freed and could be voiced earnestly and directly.

Before anyone took a stab at responding to the woman's question—*What benefit does your presence bring us?*—a man broke the prolonged silence, saying: "We do all your labor." He paused, as if waiting for somebody to inject dissent. "All of it."

"You call us criminals," he said. "People are making sacrifices for their families"—he gestured to the people sitting around him on the metal folding chairs, bundled up in jackets, all focused on his words—"so their children can have a taco."

He continued with building emotion: "We are now separated from our children and you *still* call us criminals." Many people in front of us nodded in agreement, moving others to comment on the atrocity of children torn away from their parents. This was five months before Attorney General Jeffrey Sessions gave his "zero tolerance" speech, and forced family separations became a daily feature in the news cycle. But they were talking about separation policies that long predated Trump.

Back at his State of the Union monologue, Trump was announcing his "four pillars" of immigration reform that would "fully secure the border," and end the "visa lottery" and "chain migration" while associating border-crossers—like all the people before us in the shelter—with the violent MS-13 gang.

Indeed, while an awkward tension persisted, people began to talk, and the conversation became more pregnant with possibility, creating a sort of bridge between us. Suddenly the border meant nothing. Indeed, the very conversation challenged not only the militarized borders imposed between us, but also the way they suffocate debate and discourse. We could feel, as the profound Nigerian thinker and writer Bayo Akomolafe would say, the composting of such notions. With the awkwardness came something else: an understanding that how things are named, acknowledged, and funded were choices that perpetuate unjust realities and preventable suffering. Change is also a choice, and to drive it, we need new language, one that acknowledges and asserts a sovereignty and solidarity greater than any wall. By committing to such choices, we enter what Akomolafe calls *the sanctuary*.

In conversations with me from his home in India, Akomolafe explained the difference between refuge and sanctuary. Refuge is a place where you can be safe, where safety is the goal. Sanctuary, however, is an "invitation to lose shape, to become something different." The shelter that night in Mexico felt like it was hovering in between those two spaces.

As a Nigerian immigrant living in India, Akomolafe recounted how the reality of borders and the nation-state had become a deep part of his intimate family life. His wife's father was Nigerian, and her mother Indian, Iranian, and English. "My children," he told me, "carry borders marked with the fingerprints of the nation-state." Akomolafe also told me that for him, entering the United States was often "trauma-inducing," and that every airport is also a border, a biopolitical machine that brands bodies like cattle. He told me that borders for him have always been "assemblages of violence," and for this reason, his work has been an attempt to "transgress them." The title of his gorgeously written book, *These Wilds Beyond Our Fences*, underscores this. What kind of raw and beautiful world lies beyond the fences and walls that confine not just our bodies, but also our imagination, our speech, our very humanity? The possibilities of such a world have yet to be fully imagined.

Sanctuary, says Akomolafe, is closely allied with the concept of "fugitivity," a "transgression of the plantation, borders, and the character of the nation-state, which smacks of criminality." I couldn't help but think of the sanctuary movement of the 1980s, and how its members consciously broke the law. At first pastors, parishioners, and nuns drove the cross-border movement, but as their civil disobedience ethically inspired others, universities and entire cities—sanctuary cities—rose up in resistance to the

U.S. laws prohibiting people like Juan Carlos from being in our country.

Today's sanctuary movement again offers safe space for dignified residence, especially for those who fear deportation and forced separation from their families. To Akomolafe's point, sanctuary is a place where ethical rules and human rights transcend and transgress those of the nation-state and corporate economy. But sanctuary is also a sovereign zone of wilderness and imagination beyond walls and fences, where you could steal away into "places that are not yet there, not yet dawned, not yet built, places where failure meets success...amniotic places that are still emerging."

Seen in this context, perhaps one could reframe the woman's question to us as *How can we work together? How can we build a new world together?* To continue beyond the awkward pause that followed her question was to walk beyond our own failures, to feel our preconceived notions steam in the compost, and to understand that so many voices—like those of the people before us in the shelter—cannot be left out of the discussion again.

Another man from the back of the chapel asked us: "Why is it so hard for us and so easy for you to cross the border?" There was another pause while we contemplated our own mobility in contrast to the violence of civilization's heavily policed boundaries upon the people in front of us, enforcing divisions of class, race, and in some places, religion. Again there was silence, the only sound the traffic in the Nogales night outside the chapel.

"Did Mexican officials," the man continued, "ask you for papers when you crossed the border?" One student answered no, and it came out rather reluctantly, almost as if she wished they had.

When another man began to speak, he told the group that English was his stronger language. Like many, he had come to the United States at a young age. He lived there for many decades, was married, had a child, and owned a business. As he talked, he leaned forward in his chair and spoke with an earnest tone. His expulsion from the U.S. was so fresh that he still had unhealed gashes where the handcuffs had cut into his wrists. But those were the least of his worries.

"Will I ever see my child again?" he asked the group, unable to hide his tears.

The woman in the front row asked again: "What benefit does your presence bring us?" In a way, this book is a response to that question even being voiced, a response to how walls and borders have had catastrophic consequences for the people in the shelter, and how they have become alienating and internalized for many people like us in the United States.

The sanctuary, Akomolafe says, is not a "vocation of establishing manifestos" but rather a "politics of incapacitation, a politics of composting, a politics of falling apart, and I say this as not something to fear, or something that is bad." The immigration and border apparatus is not "broken" and it does not need to be "fixed." Rather it needs to be incapacitated, it needs to fall apart, it needs to be placed into the fertile compost where answers are always emerging and shifting shape like new life in a womb.

21

And how could people best resist the border?

In the sanctuary, says Akomolafe, we will find the "fugitive spirit," the key to breaking through into something new. There is a "modest criminality," but it is "not totalizing." This is the breaking-through committed by good troublemakers like John Lewis, Fannie Lou Hamer, Martin Luther King, and cofounder of the Black Lives Matter movement Patrisse Cullors. As I listened to Akomolafe say *modest criminality*, I noticed how it both provoked and enticed my imagination. I thought of that moment in the desert with Juan Carlos, and understood that in order to move past this, transgress this, there will have to be criminality. But how do you do it modestly, with creativity, as an act of affirmation?

The elder woman, wrapping the blanket around her shoulders, looked up to ask one more question. I sensed her fugitive spirit. We had no way of knowing what Trump was saying at that precise moment. What mattered more was that we all shifted our shapes just a little. This was due to our failure to answer her first question: How will your presence benefit us? And it also perfectly set up the woman's second question, which she asked right as we were about to leave.

She was, I am convinced to this day, trying to help us find an answer to the first one: "Have you come to tear down the Berlin Wall?"

WALL SICKNESS

As always, the Border Patrol agent sat in his green-striped vehicle under the camera post at the top of the hill, next to the twenty-foot border wall. The vantage point offered a sweeping view of Nogales, from both sides of the border. I was there with a friend from Washington, D.C., and his teenage kids. We parked the car, crossed the road, and stood in front of the wall, 100 feet below the agent. At that precise moment we heard the Border Patrol vehicle's engine growl as the agent hit the gas. He kicked up gravel before he shot down the hill. At first, I thought he was heading for us, but he ripped by and skidded to a stop fifty yards past us, where a multigenerational group of seven people or so stood talking with three others on the other side of the wall. There were kids and teenagers and older people—most likely a family—conversing through the barred wall, which created the feeling of incarceration regardless of which side you are on. It was December 26, 2016, a month away from the Trump administration taking power.

The term "wall sickness" first came from the heightened feeling of anxiety suffered by German people who lived near the Berlin Wall. "It was an illness with a deep impact on my psyche," Gitta Heinrich told the BBC of her lived experience. "It was this real feeling of narrowness," one caused by the internalization of the wall into the people's psyche.

Below us, the border agent got out of his car and began barking at the group. Family members looked over at the agent warily. Indeed, he looked like a man infected with wall sickness. His exaggerated gesticulations bespoke a worldview that was enforced through him and also went beyond him, to the recruiting and training of the U.S. Border Patrol, to the spectacle of nationalism scripted into every Super Bowl broadcast, to the speeches of every U.S. president, Democrat or Republican, who has spoken of Manifest Destiny or American exceptionalism. It is a binary worldview of us versus them, exceptional versus inferior, good versus bad, innocent versus criminal, legal versus illegal, either you think exactly like us or you are the enemy. And these binaries are reinforced by the gun, the camera, the wall, and the law. The family, obviously, had breached one of those lines the U.S. Department of Homeland Security had tasked the agent to protect and preserve. Perhaps the toddler had touched the wall, but from where we stood, none of us could tell what the violation actually was.

In August 2019, *Current Affairs* editor Nathan Robinson interviewed Ezra Klein, one of the founders of Vox Media. At one point in the conversation Klein, whose father was an immigrant, says that he'd "like to see larger rates of immigration, but I don't think we can be politically stable with open borders." Klein admits that his own thinking is "unsettled," and that if he were certain that the United States could handle open borders, he would support it. Klein brings up open borders in a way that avoids stigmatizing the possibility but at the same time rejects it as impractical. I mention Klein because I think the idea of impracticality is indoctrinated through both political parties and mainstream media. Such indoctrination and discourse on borders ultimately impede any serious discussion about their function.

In Nogales, the twenty-foot wall that towered over us looked like an effort to do just that: not only impede freedom of movement, but also censor any conversation about it—or through it—the agent chastising the family being a case in point. Looking below, into Mexico, we could see the altar for 16-year-old José Antonio Elena Rodríguez, who had been killed, shot ten times in the back, by a Border Patrol agent on October 10, 2012. The modest altar, composed of a white cross decorated with yellow and orange flowers, appeared in front of a building whose drab walls were pocked with bullet holes. "They cut off his wings," José Antonio's brother Diego told me when we met at a restaurant a couple of blocks away from the altar in 2014. "He was my brother, but he was also my best friend."

To the east and to the west, we could see the U.S. border wall snake up through the hilly Nogales landscape and off into the horizon. On the Mexican side, people walked on uneven sidewalks in front of colorful buildings. Large white buses loudly drove by, arriving at their destination just south of the border wall. I thought about a friend of mine named Flaco who had been driving one of those bus routes every day for more than twenty years. Despite this, he has been unable to get a visa, and has yet to set foot in the United States.

Discussions about open borders often focus on the movements of the poor—people like Flaco, Diego, Juan Carlos, and the family berated by the Border Patrol. For these people, simply being near the border is often treated as a violation. As a result, it would not have surprised me if the agent started arresting family members as they peacefully conversed with those gathered on the Mexican side of the wall.

Perhaps it is not extreme to say that U.S. bullets enjoy an open border policy, as Border Patrol agents have shot and killed at least ninety-seven people since 2003, sometimes shooting into Mexico, and not a single person has been charged for the deaths. The bullets speak volumes as to who and what has freedom of movement and who and what does not. To begin a real conversation about a possible open border policy, therefore, it needs to be acknowledged that such a policy already exists, and not just for the 42 percent of the U.S. population who have passports and can enter 174 countries without a visa (compared to, say, the thirty-seven countries an Iraqi passport would allow you to enter). The U.S. military, intelligence agencies, and corporations all operate in a world of no borders.

They cross whatever border they please, wherever they wish, often in the lap of luxury, 35,000 feet above the spot where the Border Patrol agent was harassing this family, 35,000 feet above the vastness where people cross deserts and rough seas, 35,000 feet above the site where border guards tear gas refugees, as U.S.-trained Mexican authorities have done multiple times on the Guatemalan border since 2018.

Yet, in Juan Carlos's Guatemala—as in most other places—the situation is different. There were no border guards armed with AR-15s, tear gas, pepper spray, and concussion grenades to stop the Boston-based United Fruit Company from setting up shop there in the early twentieth century. Guatemala had no immigration forces in place to protect it from members of the Central Intelligence Agency whose covert operations instigated a military coup to protect U.S. business from hungry, landless *campesinos* in 1954. As a result of U.S. intervention, an authoritarian military dictatorship took power in Guatemala and lasted for decades. The coup happened after Guatemalan president Jacobo Árbenz announced his intention to redistribute some of United Fruit's fallow land. Today, there are no electric smart walls to stop foreign mining companies in Guatemala, even if the companies poison the water, steal land, and extract wealth. Nor are there border controls preventing foreign textile factories from setting up shop and paying people miserably low wages. Guatemala's borders are likewise open to big agribusinesses that flood markets with cheap grains, undermining local farmers. No border patrols stop the greenhouse gases from entering the biosphere, 92 percent of it emanating from rich countries, only a fraction from Guatemala, bringing droughts and storm surges and causing havoc.

"We already have open borders for people who are very wealthy or work for large corporations," historian Guadalupe Castillo told me. "Those people are free to roam and carry out whatever they need to increase their productivity, their profits."

Yet border patrols, and hence the discussions of "open borders," exclusively target the mobility of people like Juan Carlos, the undermined farmer, the underpaid textile worker, those run off their lands by mines and other megaprojects, the displaced, the dispossessed, the family simply trying to have a cross-border conversation the day after Christmas. In terms of stability, what is actually happening is precisely the opposite of what Ezra Klein asserted to Nathan Robinson. Juan Carlos is not a threatening force—a trope undergirded by a polite, yet hidden, form of white supremacy that assigns the migrant tremendous destructive power. Juan Carlos, like many others in his situation, arrives at our doorstep disheveled, thirsty, a thousand miles away from his home, and in the middle of a distant, vast, foreign desert. And he is there precisely because the world is already destabilized.

In his book *This Land Is Our Land*, Suketu Mehta opens with a story about an angry British man who berated Mehta's grandfather in 1980s London.

"Why are you here?" the man demanded. "Why are you in my country?"

Mehta's grandfather, who was born in India and spent his working life in colonial Kenya, answered, "Because we are the creditors. You took all our wealth, our diamonds. Now we have come to collect."

"We are here," Mehta's grandfather was saying, "because you were there."

❧

BELOW US IN Nogales, the agent abruptly halted his lecture and tore up the hill again, spitting gravel from his wheels. I was relieved, because you never know how such a scene might play out. Every day such displays of asymmetrical power take place, small acts of aggression that never make the news. Before long, the agent returned to his perch under the camera post, an elevated spot providing unobstructed views of the surrounding area. This whole scene would not have happened before 1994, when there was only a chain-link fence with big holes through which people would cross back and forth. According to longtime resident and musician Gustavo Lozano, back then the only worry was the occasional presence of a kid at the hole asking for pocket change. When Lozano occasionally got caught by the Border Patrol and thrown back into Mexico, there was no incarceration, no formal deportation on his record. He told me that he would often cross from Mexico into the United States to pay a bill at a department store for his mom, to play basketball with his cousins, to hang out with his family. As late as the 1980s, on holidays such as September 16—Mexican Independence Day—officials opened the borders completely and a parade zigzagged back and forth as if the international boundary simply didn't exist.

Ambos Nogales is one place that exists on both sides of the U.S.-Mexico border. *Ambos* means "both," and as the name suggests, communities on both sides of the border share deep familial, community, social, economic, and political ties. They also share common infrastructure. As Ieva Jusionyte writes in her book *Threshold: Emergency Responders on the U.S.-Mexico Border*, "extending from northern Sonora to southern Arizona, the railway, the highway, even the sewage pipeline facilitate dense ties between the two sides of the border. It becomes impossible to disentangle one town's everyday logistics from the other's." The border cannot stop the roots of trees and the vast mycelium networks symbiotically entangled with them from reaching across to the other side. At Ambos Nogales, the border is not designated by a mountain, lake, or river. This border first came into being as an imaginary line in the sand with the Gadsden Purchase in 1853, that is, if a transaction at gunpoint can be considered a "purchase." Officials from both countries put up the first permanent fence in 1918 after what was known as the Battle of Ambos Nogales. The battle resulted from spiking tensions after the implementation of passport requirements by the United States, which included limiting the number of times Mexican citizens could cross the border. Repeated shootings by U.S. Customs agents and military, including the killing of two Mexican citizens, precipitated the combat. In his book *Violent Borders*, geographer Reece Jones argues that borders are implicitly violent, often from their very inception.

Nevertheless, despite these U.S. border wars with Mexico, there is a long history of cross-border cooperation and mutual aid among the people. For example, fire units on both sides have crossed back and forth for decades in mutual assistance. Louie Chaboya, who served as the director of emergency services in Arizona's Santa Cruz County, where Nogales is located, noted to Jusionyte this underlying sense of connection uniting the communities on both sides of the divide. "In Nogales," he said, referring to this cross-border cooperation, "we are not associates. We are not business partners. We are not even friends. We are family."

In that spirit, anthropologist Josiah Heyman posed a broader question in his 1999 essay "A Border that Divides, A Border that Joins." "What if we think of Mexico and the United States as one country, unified, rather than divided by the border?" Heyman asks. "Issues often framed as contrasting the United States with Mexico

31

are better understood as the allied elites and finances of both countries (plus Canada) versus divided and somewhat anxious commoners of the entire continent."

It could also be understood in another way: For the cross-border networks of allied elites, borders are open, but for a purposely discombobulated working class on the Mexican side, borders are all but closed. The working class in the United States is told that the Mexican working class is dragging its wages down, while the allied elites move good jobs across the border without impediment.

It's a worthwhile thought experiment to imagine the world without human-imposed borders for working-class people. The Earth has existed for 4.5 billion years, humans and ancestors of humans for six million years, and civilization as we know it for only 6,000 years. Perhaps the world's astronauts sensed this as they contemplated the sweeping view of the planet and experienced a sense of interconnected global consciousness. There is a reason they cannot see the borders, mostly because human-drawn international political boundaries are artificial and new, and do not register as topography, unlike bodies of water, rivers, and mountain ranges. The border in Nogales, for example, was drawn in 1853 without any agreement from the original inhabitants of this land, the Tohono O'odham. Colonial European powers sliced up Africa during the 1883 Berlin Conference, effectively creating the borders of its modern nation-states, without consulting any African people. The Sykes-Picot agreement of 1916 divvied up the Middle East to the logic of the British and French, and not, say, the Palestinians. These artificial borders and their enforcement apparatuses are relatively new—border militarization, for example, has accelerated in the last twenty-five years—and often imposed by faraway allied elites.

In the grand scheme of things, borders now largely serve as a neocolonial scaffolding for a planet divided into exploiting and exploitable countries and peoples. They are untouchable. As an example, on one occasion Moroccan military and security personnel surrounded me and briefly confiscated my phone for simply taking pictures outside the border wall separating Morroco and the autonomous Spanish city of Ceuta. But even as they surrounded me—they were paid by the European Union to provide "security"—I realized this was the universal conditioning around borders. You are on the "sacred ground" of the nation-state, the border is its ultimate monument, humanity be damned.

So to continue the thought experiment, what if we were to allow ourselves to imagine a world without borders? What if we were to see borders not as shields, but as shackles keeping the planet in an unsustainable status quo of inequality, racial divide, and climate catastrophe?

Perhaps philosopher Michael Marder was contemplating these questions when he wrote an op-ed for the *New York Times* on March 3, 2020, titled "The Coronavirus Is Us." In his op-ed, Marder describes his version of wall sickness: "Well before the current outbreak, a global tendency to build walls and seal off national borders…had taken hold. The resurgent nationalism instigating this tendency nourishes itself on the fear of migrants and social contagion, while cherishing the impossible ideal of purity within the walled polity." Concerned with how such tendencies would complicate solving the coronavirus crisis, Marder continues the metaphor to encompass the global lockdown in which people are further divided by class. "As panic sets in," he wrote, "in some quarters, personal border closure imitates the knee-jerk political gesture: Food and medical supplies are hoarded, while the wealthiest few prepare their luxury doomsday bunkers." Marder arrives at the border's eternal paradox: "Borders are porous by definition; no matter how fortified, they are more like living membranes than inorganic walls. An individual or a state that effectively manages to cut itself off from the outside will be as good as dead."

In April 2020, political cartoonist Matt Wuerker published a cartoon of a stern general looking out from a missile-laden border barrier, as his minion spots a coronavirus floating over the wall with his binoculars. For better and worse, the virus reveals humanity's interconnection, and the inability of borders to truly partition us, even when sealed as tightly as possible. In this sense, the coronavirus becomes not only a catastrophe but also a lyrical messenger.

For Marder, it delivers a prescient message for the post-pandemic future: The coronavirus speaks to the inability of walled countries to respond to global issues such as climate catastrophe—the pandemic being but one aspect of it—and advocates for us to "learn to live in a world that is interconnected." Contemplated as one might contemplate a poem, the pandemic could be seen as a deep call to action, part of the "great turning," as deep ecology scholar Joanna Macy has written, from an industrial-growth society that relies on borders, to a more sustainable civilization for which borders are an impediment. "The most remarkable feature of this historical moment on Earth," says Macy, "is not that we are on the way to destroying the world—we've actually been on the way for quite a while. It is that we are beginning to wake up from a millennia-long sleep, to a whole new relationship to our world, to ourselves, and each other."

In this sense, we can only hope that the director for the International Institute for Environment and Development, Andrew Norton, is right to state that the lessons drawn from COVID-19 could apply also to climate change. "Strengthening recognition of our interdependence—that everyone's health is everyone else's business—could strengthen the understanding that compassion and empathy are functional traits for humanity," he writes. "The virus may lead to a deeper understanding of the ties that bind us all on a global scale." Coronavirus is thus an offering for us to reimagine borders, what they are, who they are for, who they are not for, and how humanity and the Earth will be better served without them.

↜

I BECAME AWARE of wall sickness the day I first set foot in Nogales, in January 1995. I arrived with a large army bag full of stuff and a strong desire to leave the United States for a long time. This trip was at least partly inspired by the stories I had heard throughout my childhood from my grandparents, who loved Latin America and traveled there often. My Filipina grandmother grew up speaking Spanish (along with Tagalog and English) and was always drawn to places like Mexico, Guatemala, and Peru for that reason. And my grandfather, a farmer from Penn Yan, New York, loved Mexico so much that he didn't stop going until he was in his late nineties; he would go for months at a time, long after my grandmother died. He became somewhat famous in the city of Oaxaca, partly due to his age and partly due the fact that he attempted to translate *Dante's Inferno* from the English version to Spanish. After getting off a Greyhound bus from Tucson in 1995, I saw the then freshly minted border wall for the first time. In 1994, the U.S. had yanked out the chain-link fence in Nogales and replaced it with a fifteen-foot wall made out of rust-colored military landing mats used in the Persian Gulf and Vietnam wars. The massive wall came not long after the Bill Clinton White House initiated Operation Safeguard, the Arizona sibling of Operation Gatekeeper, the most ambitious border militarization project up to that point, which further closed the border to working-class people. For me, that potent instant of political awareness would be reinforced by wandering for several months in Mexico with next to no money during an economic crisis with the peso in free-fall and a full-on uprising in the south led by the Zapatistas.

Although I'd been spurred by my grandparents' tales and descriptions, I arrived in Mexico ignorant of its history and its many indigenous cultures. When I was about to run out of money, I miraculously got a job teaching English in San Luis Potosí. It almost seems impossible to remember this now, but that first trip to Mexico was before the internet. I had no email. There were many bouts of loneliness and frustration of not being able to get the words in Spanish out or even understand at times what was going on around me. I also began to hear firsthand accounts of what is was like to cross the border from Mexico to the United States. In hindsight, I now realize that the most important skill I learned that year was the ability to see my country outside of its borders.

In 2000, my first bit of published journalism (in the *Earth First! Journal*) was a picture of the U.S. Army Corps of Engineers constructing that same metal wall between Douglas, Arizona, and Agua Prieta, Sonora. When I worked for the binational organization BorderLinks, from 2001 to 2004, I crossed back and forth between the United States and Mexico several times a week. One of the most unsettling things I witnessed during this time was the way the border regime further militarized after 9/11. This was the period when the term "homeland" went from being associated with Nazi Germany to designating the new security apparatus of the U.S. government.

From 2005 to 2009 I lived in Oaxaca, Mexico, and worked for a U.S. organization called Witness for Peace. For four years, I studied the profound consequences of the North American Free Trade Agreement (NAFTA) and the imposition of the neoliberal economic model by the International Monetary Fund and World Bank, for people living in the Mexican countryside, labor, and small businesses. The onslaught was clear in the emergence of *pueblos fantasmas*—ghost towns created by mass exoduses from Mexico to the United States. One of the most vivid responses to this was offered by Oaxacan artist Alejandro Santiago. When Santiago returned to his town after a long absence in the late 1990s, he said most people had left. "The only noise we heard when we returned, was our own. When everybody decided to migrate, everything became empty and alone. My friends were no longer there. My aunts and uncles were no longer there. My cousins were no longer there." To address this "painful absence" Santiago began re-creating "their souls," one by one, by making 2,501 clay sculptures. One day when I was walking in Oaxaca, I came upon a display of all 2,501 sculptures filling the streets, a moving rendition of the post-NAFTA war zone.

The years I was in Oaxaca were important for building the U.S. border wall. Through the 2006 Secure Fence Act, the George W. Bush administration extended the wall nearly 650 miles, trampling critical environmental and cultural heritage laws along vast stretches of border wilderness. Through SBInet (the technology plan of the Secure Border Initiative), and the advent of the "smart wall" or "virtual wall," the Bush administration further integrated sophisticated technological systems such as surveillance towers, motion sensors, and unmanned aerial vehicles. Among the areas impacted were the Buenos Aires and San Bernardino Wildlife Refuges, and Organ Pipe National Monument, including sacred indigenous sites that the Trump administration later desecrated in order to install his "big beautiful wall."

The bollards came in 2011, when construction crews removed landing mats and replaced them with the steel bars between which the family conversed that day on December 26, 2016. Indeed, U.S.

foreign policy had long been about building walls, in bipartisan fashion, and long before Trump. Anybody in doubt should look up the "McNamara Line," the surveillance-wall system deployed between North and South Vietnam, which later served as a prototype for the militarization of the U.S.-Mexico border in the early 1970s.

When the 2016 presidential campaign first thrust the wall into the news cycle, the fact that more than 650 miles of walls and barriers already existed received little mention. Perhaps it was savvy politics, for if Hillary Clinton had acknowledged preexisting walls it would have revealed that she, along with many other prominent Democrats such as Joe Biden and Barack Obama, had, in fact, voted for the Secure Fence Act of 2006. And for Donald Trump, such an admission would have undermined a core promise of his campaign. Much of the mass media followed suit. For a long time, outlets reported on Trump's wall promise as if the 650 miles of barrier were not there, and as if Clinton's opposition to the wall had been the stance of the Democratic Party all along. When it finally did begin to dawn on media that there was already a wall—it took a while—then the debate became semantic. What to call it? Was it a wall or a fence?

And then came the stories that showcased all the latest digital technologies revealing where the wall and barriers were already located, and the vast open areas where they were not. In an article titled "We looked at every mile of the U.S.-Mexico border. Now you can too—right here," *USA Today* reported that "huge stretches of border have no physical barrier." Unmentioned was the longstanding border strategy of "prevention through deterrence." How could the media fail to reveal the basic strategy that dictated how walls, barriers, and agents were deployed? It was the reason that walls were constructed in urban areas. The vast stretches of unpopulated desert were part of the initial strategy. Because crossing such vast stretches was so dangerous, they were meant to be a "mortal threat," as the Border Patrol explicitly said in its initial 1994 strategy memo.

During the 2016 presidential campaign, I did a simple online search to see if either candidate, Clinton or Trump, had ever mentioned the deterrence strategy, or the thousands of deaths it had caused. No. Nothing. Did any of the media ask them about this strategy? No. Was either candidate asked about this in any of their debates? No. Never. Not in any primary, either. And the same was true during the 2020 presidential campaign. The narrow range of Democrat/Republican discourse on borders limits public understanding, discussion, and debate. Corporate media color inside the lines drawn by the two-party system, thereby completing what Noam Chomsky deemed the "manufacturing consent" process. The U.S. border is defined by those in power, not by the people it divides.

Throughout 2020 in southern Arizona, you could hear the large trucks and machinery rumble day and night through places like Ajo, bringing supplies and thousands of construction workers to the Organ Pipe National Monument and other places along the U.S.-Mexico border. Bulldozers left chopped-up saguaros in their wake. Like a mine, wall construction demands water, lots of water, and Trump's wall project has drained the region's sacred Quitobaquito Springs. "It's unbelievable, it's just horrible, it's going down and down," says Hia-Ced O'odham leader Christina Andrews of the spring's depletion. She's been visiting the spring since childhood, and has never seen it so low. "It feels like a violation of innocence." Even as news that some of the construction workers were infected with COVID-19, and perhaps contributed to the outbreak in Arizona during June and July 2020, CBP kept claiming that the wall construction was stopping the virus.

While the Trump version of the wall now reaches thirty feet, I could not help but think of the fifteen-foot version I first saw in January 1995. For the past twenty-five years, wall sickness has only deepened and spread.

IN NOGALES, THE agent's vehicle growled again, then came roaring down the hill. I expected him to speed by us once more, but this time he came to a halt where the four of us stood. The passenger window went down. What, I wondered, was he going to do? The agent leaned toward us and said: "I know you aren't doing anything, but don't touch the wall. Don't be a bad example." He pointed down to the group. We were all white, and we were all speaking English. Apparently, we had our "membership" to the "club," terms used by political theorist Michael Walzer for exclusion and inclusion in a nation. If I read the agent's eyes correctly, he was now entirely caught up in a power struggle, deep in the wall sickness that serves as the perfect metaphor for where we are right now on the globe in the twenty-first century. He then cruised down the hill again toward the family, whose members seemed to have mastered the ability to ignore the loud, growling F-150 truck that skidded to another dramatic stop next to them.

We warily watched him approach the family, expecting him to just yell at them again. Even when nothing happens, everything happens. Behind every action is a threat of violence and pain, as the altar across the line so clearly demonstrated.

In 2014, on the anniversary of the fall of the Berlin Wall, the author of *Walls: Travels Along the Barricades*, Marcello Di Cintio, wrote, "The 'Berlin strain' of the Wall disease may have been cured 25 years ago, but wall-disease remains a global pandemic." When the Berlin Wall fell, there were fifteen border walls around the world; now there are more than seventy, including those between Israel and Occupied Palestine, India and Bangladesh, Hungary and Greece, Turkey and Syria, and Kenya and Somalia.

Billions have been spent on drones, high-tech cameras, motion sensors, war technology, night vision goggles, and an arsenal of weapons aimed at our neighbors on the border. There are drones of all sizes, including mini drones engineered with locust-like wings and others armed with facial recognition software. Entire places have become war zones just because there is a border, not because there is a war. Or perhaps the term "war" needs to be reassessed in the terms of Josiah Heyman's essay: Instead of countries blowing each other up, modern warfare consists of the militarized borders where allied elites suppress, attack, and exploit the global working class, small farmers, and indigenous people.

The thriving market for this is only enriched by a "build walls, not bridges" approach to solving everything from the climate crisis to the coronavirus. When I wrote *Border Patrol Nation* in 2014, the global homeland security market was hovering around $300 billion a year. Now the research company MarketsandMarkets projects that the homeland security and emergency market will grow 6.3 percent annually, expanding from $623.1 billion in 2020 to $846.5 billion in 2025. In 2020, Advance Market Analytics stated that, despite an economic collapse everywhere due to the pandemic and skyrocketing unemployment, the "border security system" had an "emerging hint of opportunity," and the "automated border control market" would have "astonishing growth." Still another report projected the border security market to grow at 6.1 percent, with "healthy gains" and "significant momentum."

Wall sickness is running wild. But that does not mean it is inevitable. It does not mean that we have to cooperate. Part of COVID-19's potent message is that everything can change at a moment's notice. Hierarchies can suddenly crash and reorganize. Perhaps the pandemic has brought humanity to something that has been needed for a long time: a new frontier. "Historically, pandemics have forced humans to break with the past and imagine their world anew," writes Arundhati Roy: "This one is no different. It is a portal, a gateway between one world and the next. We can choose to walk through it, dragging the carcasses of our prejudice and hatred, our avarice, our data banks and dead ideas, our dead rivers and smoky skies behind us. Or we can walk through lightly, with little luggage, ready to imagine another world. And ready to fight for it."

As I looked at the family one last time that day, I pondered that there are many things that elude the eye because they are below the surface, like tree roots that entangle with each other in ways that are difficult to imagine as we view a forest. In his book *The Songs of Trees*, ecologist David George Haskell writes, "Tree songs emerge from relationship. Although tree trunks seemingly stand as detached individuals, their lives subvert this atomistic view. We're all—trees, humans, insects, birds, bacteria—pluralities." Haskell continues, "Our ethic must therefore be one of belonging, an imperative made all the more urgent by the many ways that human actions are fraying, rewiring, and severing biological networks worldwide."

It matters little that militarized border enforcement prowls the surface. Solidarity happens underground. In storms, trees often stand together linked by their intertwined roots. For a moment, that seemed to be what was happening with the family. The agent yelled, we could hear his voice from where we stood, but the family paid him no heed, as if he were simply a passing storm that, with time, would just go away.

It is possible to subvert the walls across the globe as the roots of humanity connect in wild solidarity, resistance, Akomolafe's fugitive spirit, imagination, and love. The bridges already exist. Giving them voice is the first step toward transforming the walls of division into pathways of interconnection. "Walls turned sideways," writes Angela Davis, "are bridges."

When the Berlin Wall turned in 1989, it was "the emotional climax of unloading, the cathartic breaking through of the unconscious," East German psychotherapist Hans Joachim Maaz wrote. "The emotional blockage unclogged, the repressed came to the surface and the parts that had been split apart, united." When power's wall turned sideways, the people's bridge appeared.

MANIFEST DISMANTLING

IN 2008, PIVLI Takala took her seat as a new employee of Deloitte—a global consulting company that now has become one of the primary contractors for the U.S. Department of Homeland Security—and began to stare into space. When other employees asked her what she was doing, first she said "brain work." Then she said she was working on her thesis. If that didn't gall her co-workers, the day she simply rode the elevator up and down all day did. When her colleagues asked where she was going, she said nowhere. Her co-workers started to shoot around emails. Her "utter inactivity" was perplexing.

But there was something more, author Jenny Odell tried to explain in her book *How to Do Nothing*. It was also an act of interrogation. By doing nothing, Takala—who was a performance artist—was actually posing uncountable questions. According to Odell, this sort of questioning has profound effects. The act of "refusing or subverting an unspoken custom" reveals "its often-fragile contours…. For a moment, the custom is shown to be not the horizon of possibility, but rather a tiny island in a sea of unexamined alternatives."

As legend has it, around the year 400 BCE, Diogenes roamed the streets of ancient Athens holding a lamp in broad daylight. When asked what he was doing, he responded that he was looking for a "human being" or "an idea of humanity." (This is usually translated "an honest man.") Diogenes, like Pivli Takala, was interrogating the unquestioned rules by which we live. According to Odell, Diogenes was actually showing his conviction that "every 'sane' person in the world was actually insane for heeding any of the customs upholding a world of greed, corruption, and ignorance."

The simple questions voiced that night in the Nogales sanctuary were like those of Diogenes, shining a light and giving birth to yet more questions. Demanding to abolish the border is as unthinkable to many people today as it once was to ask to abolish slavery. The simple act of questioning is the first step in the process of rethinking, and potentially transforming, the world.

Like Diogenes, Irene Morales used to wander the streets of Nogales in the early morning hours. Irene was a nun from Colima, Mexico, and I knew her from my years working at BorderLinks in the early 2000s. Irene was the type of nun with whom you could drink a beer and spend an afternoon singing Latin American protest songs. We went to concerts together sometimes, including one by the great Mexican band Café Tacvba. When she told me that she woke up every day at 4:30 a.m., I immediately thought that it was to pray, since she had a small chapel in her Nogales house that she shared with two other nuns. But her answer was a swift no, it was not to pray. "At least not in the way you are thinking." She got up to go outside. She walked the unpaved, hilly, sometimes very steep streets at the hour when thousands of people were commuting to the factories in dented white buses (there are nearly 100 *maquilas*—factories—in Nogales, mainly serving U.S. companies) where it took a half day's work to afford a gallon of milk. Irene walked among the street cleaners, the garbage collectors, the houses first put together with wooden pallets and cardboard and then reinforced with cement blocks. She told me this as a matter of fact. She did it to connect with *el pueblo*—the people. She did it to learn. She did it, she said, to listen. She did it to forge deeper solidarity. Irene seemed to embody the Sufi poet Hafiz's words: "How do I listen to others? As if everyone were my teacher, speaking to me (their) cherished last words."

When I think of a "bridge," the first thing I think of is a physical object connecting one geographical place to another. But bridges may also be emotional, psychological, and spiritual structures. The concept of a bridge could even include a forest's vast underground web of tree roots and mycelial networks, anything that connects one thing to another.

For years I have wondered what would happen if a group of people simply showed up at the wall with chain saws and just began taking it down. After all, it is an impediment to connection, its very removal is the creation of a bridge. What would happen if they went right up to the border wall and let them rip? Would the thick steel bars topple easily, or would they hold stubbornly like an entrenched idea? The border wall is as much about the future as it is about the past and present. Maybe, then, by abolishing the wall, we could see there are 1,000 other possible futures waiting to bloom.

Near the end of *How to Do Nothing*, Odell describes the 1872 painting "American Progress" by John Gast. The painting depicts Manifest Destiny, the idea that white settler-colonialists pushing west through indigenous territories were not just a civilizing force, but blessed and ordained to act by higher forces. In the painting, a white female deity dressed like a Greek goddess strides westward, trampling "hundreds of species and thousands of years worth of knowledge," Odell writes. This westward expansion was the origin of today's U.S. territorial borders. Along these lines, Odell introduces a new concept, one very much in line with Takala's refusal and Diogenes's fugitive spirit: Manifest Dismantling. Manifest Dismantling would purposely undo the damage of Manifest Destiny by reckoning with its assault on indigenous civilization and the ecosystem. Odell reminds readers that when human-created dams are torn down, nature often recovers from the damage quickly. Likewise, should the 700 miles of walls and barriers that now exist along the U.S.-Mexico border be abolished, not only would freedom of movement for people be restored, but the organic habitats damaged by the wall would

be able to recover. The saguaros and mesquites would return to the scarred land; pronghorns, jaguars, and gray wolves would freely roam once again. Dismantling the wall, like dismantling a dam, opens the possibility for rewilding. By abolishing the wall, humanity uncovers the bridge, and through forging new solidarities we have the opportunity to become something new. As modern-day abolitionist Ruth Wilson Gilmore says, our task is not simply to tear down an unjust institution. "Abolition is about presence," says Gilmore, "not absence. It's about building life-affirming institutions."

In the meantime, life-negating laws and institutions such as the prison and the wall continue to control, divide, and diminish. "If the law is of such a nature that it requires you to be an agent of injustice to another, then I say break the law," said Henry David Thoreau, who famously refused to pay taxes to the U.S. government to protest a war with Mexico that ultimately redrew the U.S.-Mexico boundary. Thoreau takes it even further, and speaks of a higher law similar to the vision of the astronauts looking upon the Earth from space, where affinities become linked to a global consciousness rather than a specific country, class, or race. Indeed, if enough people abided by higher law, rather than "continuing to play the game," as Odell puts it, "then the game might actually change for once."

On September 16, 2020, Tohono O'odham members Nellie Jo David and Amber Ortega heard the rumble of wall construction teams when they were going to the sacred Quitobaquito

Springs to pray. When they saw their land being desecrated, their response was immediate. David managed to get into the bucket of one of the machines and Ortega blocked another. "We knew in our hearts that they were going to dig," David told reporter Ryan Devereaux of *The Intercept*. Perhaps they were in the same place where a group of surveyors and soldiers arrived in the mid-nineteenth century to determine, without consulting the O'odham, the new U.S. border with Mexico. Back then, a baffled O'odham elder explained that O'odham land went hundreds of miles in all directions and that their border line made no sense. In 2020, David and Ortega held their ground for more than an hour, even as dozens of armed Border Patrol agents and Park rangers arrived to arrest them. The forces of Manifest Destiny have not changed, even though nearly two centuries have passed. The forces of Manifest Dismantling, however, are now arriving en masse.

When millions of people took to the streets in thousands of U.S. cities to protest police violence against black people in June and July of 2020, we saw that underground solidarities can become visible with little notice. "We must rethink our society, from policing to the Supreme Court," author and academic Keeanga-Yamahtta Taylor said on *Democracy Now!* in September 2020, "and now it is time to throw it all open for discussion, throw it all open for debate, and that is an opportunity to rethink the society we want to live in." There are 1,000 unexamined alternatives to be imagined.

SHAPE-SHIFTING

WHEN THE GREEN-STRIPED U.S. Border Patrol vehicle cruised by us on Puerto Rico's two-lane coastal highway between Aguada and Rincón, I was struck with a surge of investigative curiosity. I asked my four-year-old son, William, if he wanted to follow it. I wanted to see with my own eyes what the U.S. Department of Homeland Security was doing on the shores of the Mona Strait. On the other side of the strait, about 250 miles away, was the island of Hispaniola, from which many Dominicans and Haitians have braved the choppy waters in makeshift boats en route to Puerto Rico.

There was no hesitation from William. His answer was a resounding *yes*. He wanted to follow the "green man," his term for Border Patrol. Although she could not yet talk, it appeared that Sofia, my one-year-old, was also game. With no one else in the car to consult, we made the decision. We were going to do to the Border Patrol agents what they usually did to everyone else: pursue, monitor, and surveil them. And because of this, unbeknownst to me at the time, we would witness a tragedy.

It was jarring to see the Border Patrol so far from our home in southern Arizona. But it shouldn't have been a surprise. I knew from years of research that the Border Patrol was everywhere in the United States, in its semi-colonies and territories, and in countries all over the world. But I was still surprised. We had been on the *isla* for six days, and every day we saw them, sometimes parked, sometimes patrolling, sometimes walking around. Even in the house where we were staying in Aguada, where we could hear the absorbing ancient

52

night songs of the coqui frogs from an adjacent pond, I was wrong to think we were far from this omnipresent surveillance apparatus. Right past the pond and through some tall trees was a lofty U.S. Navy surveillance tower buzzing with red blinking lights. If it hadn't been scouring the Mona Strait for undocumented and displaced people, I'd be tempted to say it had a festive look.

On day two of our stay, we watched an agent in a forest-green uniform walk into the Rincolini bakery to use the bathroom. The officer was weighed down by a belt that held a handgun, mace, and a billy club. And precisely that morning, after what seemed to be a tranquil coffee overlooking the now still and silent pond, a blue-striped Customs and Border Protection helicopter ripped through the sky overhead, traveling along the phenomenally damaged coastline whose eroding beaches were still scarred by Hurricane Maria's catastrophic 2017 surge.

Back on the coastal highway, we remained in hot pursuit of the agent. Go faster, William encouraged from his car seat in the back. The words BORDER PATROL were freshly painted in green on the back of his vehicle. It seemed new and shiny in comparison with the rattletraps driven by islanders and surfers. A white square gadget was mounted on top of the vehicle. I wouldn't have given it a thought, but I saw it moving. I had thought it might be a spotlight, but now I wondered if it was a camera, or maybe both.

With adrenaline swirling in the car and William yelling happily, I sped down the same damaged coastline, trying to catch up to the agent. Around us, the destruction from Maria was everywhere, even though two years had passed since the life-altering storm had struck. It wasn't just that there was no more beach; there were still uprooted trees scattered on the ground like sticks, torn from the earth by 160-mph winds. On this overcast day we could see patches of unrecovered, leafless trees, and other barren swaths, razed like logging clearcuts by one of the worst climate disasters ever to hit Puerto Rico, or even planet Earth.

Rushing down the road after the Border Patrol seemed surreal, a foray into a twenty-first-century dystopia where an intensifying climate crisis meets a multibillion-dollar surveillance state—a dystopia soon to be intensified, with the inception of the COVID-19 plague only two weeks away.

The kids were into the chase; even Sofia was squealing with delight. It was exhilarating, and we were yelling in communion as I hit the gas harder until we were just behind the Border Patrol vehicle. All this was occurring despite the white surveillance gadget that I was now convinced was spinning around and peering into our car from the rear of the agent's vehicle.

What would the agents do if they realized we were following them? Would they stop us? Lecture us? Arrest us? Incarcerate us? Shoot at us? Contemplating such possibilities was the nature of this asymmetrical surveillance system in which, according to French philosopher Michel Foucault, the common person "is seen, but does not see." In such a system, says Foucault, our relation to power is only as "an object of information, never a subject in communication."

Despite the panopticon, having my kids with me actually reduced my anxiety. William, remembering what the Border Patrol was doing back home in Arizona, asked: "Do they want to build a border wall?"

"Yes," I said, "but it's different here in Puerto Rico."

William didn't care about the differences. "We're going to smash the border wall," he said with decisive finality. Then, after a celebratory pause: "And after we smash the wall, we are going to turn it into bikes." William uttered these words as if pulverizing the wall with his voice, transforming the divider into a thing of freedom and play.

William's distrust of the "green men" began long before that moment in Puerto Rico. During an August 2019 visit to the twenty-foot bollard border wall separating Imperial Beach, California, from Mexico, William saw people waving at us from the other side of the bars in Tijuana, and he naturally began to run toward them to say hi. The foamy waves of the Pacific rolled in and coursed through the bars of the wall in such a rhythmic way that I thought if extra-terrestrials saw it, they might think it was some sort of grandiose musical instrument, not a "point of contention." Without the wall, the border would be undetectable, but the surfers riding the waves on the boundary line wouldn't have had as much fun antagonizing the Border Patrol agent up on the hill who kept blasting his horn at them as they slid back and forth between the countries. We were also near the very place where Palestinian artist Khaled Jarrar had been able to pry loose a bollard, like one does a loose tooth. Much like William wanting to turn the wall into bikes, Jarrar sculpted it into

a ladder that he eventually placed near the border wall in Ciudad Juárez, Mexico. The alchemy that William sensed was possible, the Palestinian artist actually accomplished. The physical material used to build the wall could be used for something else entirely. It was a practical political project.

William ran toward the waving people on the Tijuana side of the wall. As he did, he must have crossed an invisible line in the mind of the agent on the hill who immediately blared his metallic horn (the first time, perhaps, for somebody other than the surfers) and then said something through an intercom in a loud, disembodied voice that stopped William in his tracks. From that moment on, William wanted nothing further to do with the "green men," nor the wall.

William's imaginative ability to shape-shift intensified. Where one sees a border wall, he sees a thousand bikes, train tracks, or playgrounds yearning to be built. Though not shape-shifting in its traditional sense, the process of changing the world around us is ultimately the process of transforming ourselves. Children, like artists and revolutionaries, see things not only as they are, but as what they can become. Like Jarrar, who on another occasion pounded with a hammer and chisel on the cement wall that bisected Jerusalem, then melted the cement chunks and turned them into sculptures, William recognized many other utilitarian possibilities for materials used for border walls. As if on cue, as we walked away from the agent and back down the beach, we found some discarded cement DHS barriers, and William saw their usefulness as a urinal. As the pee splattered on the cement, it was obvious William was doing this innocently. He simply saw the chunk of wall as something else entirely.

Psychologist Ellen Langer describes "mindlessness" as the state in which a person processes information without any reflection. She writes that "when we accept an impression or a piece of information at face value, with no reason to think critically about it…that impression settles unobtrusively in our mind." Because of this, "the mindless individual is *committed* to one predetermined use of information, and other possible uses or applications are not explored."

When used without critical reflection, terms like "border security," while giving an illusion of protection, serve to reinforce an us/them mentality.

Back in Puerto Rico, I noticed that the Border Patrol vehicle in front of us visibly thumped over something. At first I couldn't tell what it was. Then, from under the vehicle, a green iguana appeared. It looked up from the asphalt, one black eye blinking, with a beautiful, ancient face. I noticed, instantly, that the Border Patrol vehicle had smashed its long tail into the pavement and rendered the animal immobile. The iguana was still alive, but frozen, wounded, suffering, and stuck on the road. To our right, the eroded beach spoke the story of sea-level rise, surges, and future storms. I swerved to the left to avoid the iguana. At first, I wanted to stop, remove the iguana from the road. Then I realized it was useless; the iguana was as good as dead.

"What was that?" William asked.

We were behind the Border Patrol vehicle again. I knew that it could have been an accident that the agent didn't see the iguana. That the agent didn't mean to hit the iguana. That the agent didn't mean to smash its tail. Perhaps the agent was attending to matters of national security. Staring off into the Mona Strait for Dominicans or Haitians. Or maybe the agent just didn't care.

"What was that?," William asked again.

"An iguana," I said.

We had been on the lookout for iguanas all week. There was a sudden silence in the back.

I didn't know what to say about the iguana, but what I was thinking went far beyond the animal. I felt that this minor tragedy was a glimpse into the future for my children's generation, one of border patrols and climate change and dead or suffering iguanas, where the ransacked coasts are patrolled instead of rehabilitated, where life is diminished instead of celebrated, where people are threats instead of treasures. Then we came to a crossroads. The agent turned south, toward Mayaguez. We went the other way, back to Aguada. At that point, even the crossroads had a symbolic resonance. As I drove back, I couldn't get the iguana out of my mind. I found myself dwelling on a report I had just read about how global populations of mammals, birds, fish, amphibians, and reptiles had declined 68 percent from 1970 to 2016, a time period in which border budgets had exploded. In 2019, other reports stated that a million plant and animal species were on the verge of extinction. Out with the endless varieties of iguanas, and in with the endless varieties of surveillance equipment.

As the woman in the Nogales sanctuary said, tearing down the walls is necessary, but, as was becoming evident, only as one part of a much larger, long-term project. As we passed the razed hills and the flattened leafless trees cut down by Hurricane Maria (as well as the flowering tamarind trees emerging since then), I reflected on the constant presence of the U.S. security state, from bobbing Coast Guard cutters in San Juan to the surveillance tower to this agent who had just run over an iguana—and William's ability to see bicycles in border walls. Such ability is the light of our humanity, an understanding that not only do things not have to be the way they are, but there is no way that they can stay the same. As the Cuban singer Silvio Rodriguez expresses in *Resumen de Noticias*, his 1978 song, "*Yo he preferido hablar de cosas imposibles. Porque de lo posible se sabe demasiado*"—"I have long preferred to speak of the impossible. Because of the possible, we already know way too much." Indeed, we have reached the moment where it is imperative to think the unthinkable. It was time, as William was teaching me, to shape-shift.

There is a 2018 picture of 15-year-old Greta Thunberg sitting in front of the Swedish parliamentary building, completely alone. There was no media presence, no social media amplifying her message, not even one other person sitting next to her. She was not, at that moment, famous. On one side of her was the sign SKOLSTREJK FÖR KLIMATET, and on the other a purple backpack. Noting the urgency of the climate crisis and the lack of policies to change it, on

October 31, 2018, she declared, "We can't save the world by playing by the rules. Because the rules have to be changed. Everything needs to change. And it has to start today. So, everyone out there: It is time for civil disobedience. It is time to rebel." One year later, on September 22, 2019, four million people joined her school strike.

It takes courage and heart to break convention, to speak out, to stand up to protect a sacred spring or call for a strike. The world can and does change when we take those first steps together. As Edgar Villanueva, an enrolled member of the Lumbee Tribe of North Carolina, writes in his book *Decolonizing Wealth*: "The principle of All My Relations means that everyone is at home here. Everyone has a responsibility in making things right. Everyone has a role in the process of healing, regardless of whether they caused or received more harm. All our suffering is mutual. All our healing is mutual. All our thriving is mutual."

TWO

A HIGHER LAW

This work has the potential to be radical because it's so embodied. That is, there is nothing abstract about immigration debates when someone is sitting in front of you with their child. In that moment, the political vortices of everything that brought the person here collide with people's reclaiming of their ordinary humanity. That juxtaposition produces a truth so searing that it penetrates into the calcium of your bones and rearranges your molecules. It makes you want to tear down hierarchies.

—Elizabeth Oglesby

ONE DAY IN 2008, Border Patrol Agent Brendan Lenihan was working alone in southern Arizona when he received a dispatch to investigate a motion sensor that had been triggered nearby. The U.S. borderlands with Mexico hold thousands of hidden sensors, and only Border Patrol knows where they are. Lenihan went up a narrow road into the Las Guijas Mountains, named for the 19th-century Spanish miners who searched for gold there. The closest community to him was Arivaca, Arizona, a small unincorporated town located about eleven miles north of the border. Its population was concerned about the increasing number of people entering the town in distress or injured, or dying in the surrounding desert. When Homeland Security installed a checkpoint in 2006, people from Arivaca could not leave their community—to go to the grocery store, to go to the doctor, to go to school—on any paved road without going through a Border Patrol blockade. In a few years this imposition would cause a great deal of activism, including protests at the checkpoints themselves, and a petition signed by more than half of Arivaca's 600 people demanding the blockades' removal.

Lenihan's green-striped truck scraped against mesquite branches as he drove up the narrowing trail between large rock faces. As he pushed farther in, he didn't know what to expect. Sometimes the sensors expose people attempting to cross the border, other times they reveal stray cattle. The trail came to an end by an abandoned mine shaft close to the top of the ridgeline. With nowhere left to drive, Lenihan parked and got out of his car. He paused to survey the sweeping view of the San Luis Mountains, the Altar Valley, and the Buenos Aires Wildlife Refuge, home to fleet-footed pronghorns, pumas, and more than 300 species of birds. To the west was Baboquivari Mountain with its pronounced, vivid peak—the region where I met Juan Carlos. Agent Lenihan told me it was a "beautiful spot," as if he could have just sat there, staring out onto the borderless landscape, for the rest of his shift. He could see not only hundreds of miles, but millions of years, if you considered the lifetimes of the mountain ranges.

"Seen from space," wrote retired astronaut Scott Joseph Kelly in 2020, following in the global-consciousness footsteps of his predecessors, "the Earth has no borders." Among the "side effects of seeing Earth from the perspective of space, at least for me, is feeling more compassion for others." Kelly's words seemed to foreshadow what Brendan Lenihan was about to experience, one of the most powerful stories of empathy I've ever heard.

Roman Krznaric, author of the book *Empathy: Why It Matters, and How to Get It*, argues that human beings have the ability to see the world through other people's eyes, and feel the world through their experiences. The ability to empathize is an innate sense, like sight or smell, and, like a muscle, it strengthens with use and atrophies with neglect. Krznaric is not talking about watered-down versions of empathy designed for consumption—often used by politicians for political gain, or corporations to sell products—but rather a vehicle of great transformative power that leads ultimately to solidarity.

What made Lenihan's experience even more notable was that one of the four blockades to empathy, Krznaric writes, is prejudice. And the definition he lays out could have come directly from a Border Patrol training manual: "[To] make snap judgments based on first impressions, and casually project our biases and preconceptions onto people while knowing very little about their lives."

After taking in the view, Lenihan continued to investigate what may have triggered the sensor. There were "all kinds of footprints," he said, fresh footprints that crossed the road in front of him and then went up into a saddle on the ridgeline. He figured that a small group was about forty-five minutes ahead of him, the exact time it took him to get up the trail. He quickly made a plan. He would call for help, then hike quickly to the north side of the ridgeline to cut off the group in the valley below.

Just as he was getting started, the situation changed. A man appeared out of a ravine on the other side of the road and ran toward Agent Lenihan, frantically waving his arms and calling for help. Lenihan had trouble with the rapid-fire, panicked Spanish, but he could understand that a relative of the man was in trouble. Trained to make quick, snap judgments, Lenihan quickly scanned the man and the surroundings. He told me that the first thing he noticed was that the man had on nice boots, and that the man seemed "comfortable" in the terrain. He seemed athletic, muscular but not burly. Then Lenihan noticed something else.

"He had kind eyes," Lenihan told me. "I trusted his face."

Lenihan grabbed his heavy assault rifle and slung it over his back. "Show me what's going on," he said. Rogelio, as Lenihan would soon learn was his name, led him to a remote spot a few minutes' hike from where he had parked. On the sandy ground in the wash at the bottom of the ravine he saw Rogelio's young brother, Roberto, lying in his cousin Miguel's lap. Miguel, who seemed older than Rogelio and Roberto, was propping up the young man's head, gently rocking him, as if he were a child. Miguel smiled sofly, but said nothing to Lenihan. Around them were tortillas and a few jugs of water. Roberto's eyelids were closed. When they opened, his eyes were rolled back, only the whites visible.

Roberto needed immediate medical attention. Lenihan's thoughts turned fast and staccato. There was no way that they would be able to land a helicopter in the ravine. But the turnout on the road where he had parked his truck might be a good place. He called dispatch and requested air support for a medical evacuation.

The three of them had to team up to get Roberto out of the ravine. The boy had a stocky build. He was difficult to lift. Then he began to vomit. The rising sun burned down on them. They tried different ways to hold Roberto. "I was worried about him choking," Lenihan said. By now, they were sweating profusely. Finally, Lenihan braced arms with Rogelio, forming a bridge, a sort of stretcher to carry Roberto in a lying position. As their grip started to slip due to sweat and strain, the agent felt the heavy AR-15 dig into the carotid artery in his neck.

Their hold on Roberto continued to slip until Lenihan and Rogelio found themselves holding hands. When Lenihan felt Rogelio's callused hands, everything started to shift. The situation became "strangely intimate." The boy continued vomiting, black bile oozing slowly out of him like lava. The heavy vomit rolled down Roberto's chest. It rolled onto Lenihan's and Rogelio's arms as they clasped hands. The Border Patrol agent looked down at Roberto. Then Lenihan was no longer Lenihan. Intimately touching Rogelio's hands, for a moment he became Rogelio. He began to see the boy as if he were his own brother.

"It was a bond," Lenihan told me, "that was strangely deep."

During Lenihan's training for the U.S. Border Patrol, a drill sergeant yelled at him for sixty-nine days. In role-playing scenarios, he was assaulted and beaten as part of his training. Police-grade pepper spray was shot into his eyes as he did jumping jacks. He underwent seventy-seven hours of intensive firearms training, often using outlines of human torsos and heads as targets. The lines of good and bad, innocent and evil, legal and illegal were drawn clearly every day.

Yet when Agent Brendan Lenihan clasped Rogelio's callused hands in their common struggle to carry Roberto to safety, for a fleeting moment, the border was gone. With it went his uniform, badge, laws, and gun. In their place was a bridge, across which he could see and feel the world from Rogelio's side—his longing, his love, his family, and his anguish and despair. As the black bile continued to ooze out of the boy's mouth, Rogelio looked at Brendan with a terrified grimace. Then the radio crackled, calling Lenihan back to the U.S. Border Patrol once again. For Roberto, in the agent's arms, the border had never left. It continued to kill him.

The helicopter wouldn't be able to safely land by the car. They landed instead at a nearby clearing. As Brendan snapped back to protocol, the previous moment remained with him—a transformative moment, a bridge to another reality. "I usually have hands-on contact with someone just long enough to put on handcuffs and send them away, and there I was, holding hands with someone I'd usually just arrest."

"As a border patrol agent," Lenihan said, "you have a muted sense of empathy because you see so much all the time that you just don't know how to cope."

Brendan's empathy transcended Border Patrol training and culture. No More Deaths, a humanitarian aid organization that compiled thousands of testimonies of people who were abused during short-term detention, charged the Border Patrol with producing "a culture of cruelty" in a 2011 report. Sean C. Chapman, the lawyer of Agent Matthew Bowen, who in 2019 faced federal charges for hitting a Guatemalan man, Antolín López Aguilar, with his Border Patrol truck, gave a glimpse into this culture during the trial. Chapman was forced to explain the trove of text messages from Bowen uncovered by prosecutors, one of which described migrants as "disgusting subhuman shit unworthy of being kindling for a fire." Throughout his text conversations, Bowen used the word "tonk"—onomatopoeia for the sound of an agent's flashlight striking a person's head. Chapman made a startling claim, throwing the "bad apple" narrative to the wind: In Bowen's defense, he stated that the denigrating language used by his client was "commonplace throughout the Border Patrol's Tucson sector, and that it is part of the agency's culture." All of this underscores what Greg Grandin wrote in his Pulitzer Prize–winning book, *The End of the Myth*: The U.S. Border Patrol has been "a frontline instrument of white supremacist power" since its founding in 1924.

Over the years, I have interviewed many agents in many settings, from government offices to private homes. While these interviews and other reporting confirm the existence of a top-down, violent, and dehumanizing culture among border enforcement personnel, it is much more difficult to generalize about the agents themselves. Talking one on one, I have met agents whose attitudes span a wide spectrum. For example, one agent attempted to justify using snipers to shoot at "aliens" if they were suspected of smuggling. When I asked the agent how he could identify who was a smuggler, he replied that smugglers have phones, and pointed to his hip.

71

Another agent I interviewed was an expert marksman in charge of conducting trainings at a shooting range, but admitted that he hated guns. He told me he had vowed to write a scathing account of the Border Patrol when he retired. A former agent was a thoughtful historian who, while working for the Border Patrol, spoke critically about U.S. drug laws and advocated for legalization. His mother was from Chihuahua, Mexico, and he joined the Border Patrol after he lost his job at Circuit City when the company went under in 2007. But the Border Patrol job did not last either. His pride in his Mexican ancestry and his advocacy for marijuana legalization ended up drawing the attention of those in higher command, who fired him. Even though 50 percent of the Border Patrol agents are Latinx, when they show pride in their heritage, if they dare, their loyalty to the United States is questioned.

After a long interview at another agent's house, the man invited me to join him for dinner. His openness and hospitality, as with many of my other interviewees, challenged my preexisting expectations and biases. Becoming sympathetic to Border Patrol agents, even liking some of them, has had an odd effect on me. I began to see that the agents were the most visible elements, yet only a small part of a much bigger system that included paper pushers, policy-makers, politicians, and private corporations that sell bullets and weapons and high-tech cameras for a profit. Focusing solely on the agents obscures this vast and hidden world of the border-enforcement apparatus— a world funded by everybody in the United States who pays taxes. And through taxes, my own connection to this apparatus is direct.

I pay the agents' salaries, I pay for the drones, I pay for the ground-sweeping radar systems and aerostats, I pay for the detention centers, I pay the administrators who sign into policy the most heinous treatment of our fellow human beings. I play a part in perpetuating a system that sustains a world of catastrophic inequalities where 2,153 billionaires have more money than 4.6 billion people—60 percent of the world population. Our taxes enforce such hierarchies of inequality and determine who can move across certain lines of division and who cannot, who serves and who is served. Individual agents are cogs in a complex machine made of disposable parts. If they do not sufficiently conform to this system, if they do not conform to the militant enforcement of U.S. borders, they get fired. This grander theater spares no one, including the agents, in its inhumanity. And, as Francisco Cantú writes about in *The Line Becomes a River*, the theater doesn't spare the agents from the nightmares and the trauma.

Another blockade to empathy fits right into this. According to Krznaric, it is "the human tendency to obey authority." He uses the example of one of the administrators of the Holocaust, Adolf Eichmann, who claimed no responsibility for his actions during his 1961 trial. Eichmann's defense was that he was simply "doing his job." Part of that job was to abide by the Nazi classifications of people such as *Untermenschen*—subhumans—the category given to Jews, Roma, Slavs, and people of color. It is also worth remembering that Adolph Hitler praised U.S. immigration law in 1936 by saying that the United States was "making progress toward a healthy racial order." As political theorist

Hannah Arendt famously pointed out, there was nothing psychopathic about Eichmann: He was a fairly typical person who "did his duty" and "not only obeyed orders but obeyed the law." He was, Arendt said, "terribly and terrifyingly normal." The same is true for most of the Border Patrol agents I've met and interviewed. Once, in a weekly birthing class, I was awkwardly paired for weeks with an agent who was also expecting a child. When we shared what we did, he said he worked for the Border Patrol. I said I wrote about the border. And we just left it at that. Most agents want to enjoy their days off with their families and friends. Yet all must obey the top-down command structure. If they do not obey authority, they lose their jobs.

When I first met Brendan Lenihan, I immediately liked him. He was soft-spoken and often chose his words with a thoughtfulness and reflection that eluded many smartphone-obsessed civilians. When he shared with me some of his journal entries, they reminded me of Cormac McCarthy's writing, a far cry from some of the warstory literature written by other Border Patrol agents. It was through Lenihan's journals that I first learned of his encounters with Rogelio, Roberto, and Miguel.

Lenihan and the group reached the clearing before other agents arrived. At that point, he was focused on keeping Roberto alive, even as he thought there was little hope. Empathy made him superhuman. When Roberto's breathing slowed and appeared to stop, Lenihan got a plastic CPR mask, put it on Roberto's face, and began to breath air into his lungs. Streams of blood and black bile continued to ooze out of the boy. Lenihan started to ingest Roberto's bile and vomit, but that no longer mattered.

Within minutes the Border Patrol chopper landed down the hill, and a group of emergency medical technicians rushed to the scene. They started to pump oxygen into Roberto's lungs with a buzzing machine. Lenihan could see the lungs inflate and contract as if the boy had started breathing again. He had a brief surge of excitement and relief that Roberto might make it.

He asked the EMT, "Is the boy alive?"

"No," the EMT told him. "The lungs always do that. The boy," he said, "is dead." That would make Roberto one of 180 people known to have died crossing into Arizona that year. Since the design of the deterrence policy forces people into desolate places, corpses are often difficult to locate. Thousands of families turn to organizations such as the Colibri Center for Human Rights that use forensic data to help search for lost loved ones. And although the remains of more than 8,000 people have been found in the U.S.-Mexico borderlands since 1998, anthropologist Jason DeLeon, author of *The Land of Open Graves*, estimates that, if you were to include the deaths of people traveling in Mexico, the count might be three to ten times higher.

When agents go off to drink and commiserate, they called it "choir practice." When Brendan's shift ended he was deeply shaken, and he headed to a bar to drink it off. Other agents tried to console him. They reminded him, according to Lenihan, that it was all part of the "border game." But it was hard for him to move beyond the fact that earlier that day a boy had died in his arms, a boy he had seen more as a brother. The next day his supervisor called him while he was home in his apartment. The supervisor understood that Lenihan was deeply troubled by the death.

"Don't worry," the supervisor said, "they were drug mules."

When Brendan recounted this story to me for the first time, he paused at this statement. Perhaps he remembered the faces of the boy and his brother and cousin.

"What did I care if they were drug mules?" he said.

Later that very evening, the smell of marijuana wafted up to his apartment from somewhere below.

"What was I even doing?" Brendan asked me, his voice filled with emotion.

ONE OF THE things that Brendan related to me about the transformative nature of his encounter was how holding hands with Rogelio and connecting with Roberto turned his thoughts to his own brother. "It could've been me if I were born on the other side of the border and I didn't have any options. I can imagine myself and my brother trying to cross. I can see us saying to each other, 'Let's go, they're not going to let us in any other way. Let's go.'"

"Did it matter to you," I asked during an interview with Lenihan in May 2020, years after he left the Border Patrol, "that it turned out that they were trying to smuggle in drugs?"

"To me," said Brendan, "it doesn't make a difference. They just seemed like regular guys. And who knows what kind of job I would have had if I grew up with them in their situation in life. It could have been me. I could have been one of them."

"What about the marijuana they were hauling?"

"Somebody died trying to sneak drugs into our country, and I went out there and had this strange and traumatic experience trying to both stop them and help them. And now my neighbor is smoking the very thing I am trying to stop. There is an element of absurdity to it all."

With the pungent smell of *mota* in his own apartment complex, one of the justifications for his job went up in smoke. And perhaps that is just the beginning of the absurdity. Most illicit drugs are not smuggled through the desert, as Rogelio, Roberto, and Miguel were allegedly doing. As much as 90 percent, as reported by the U.S. federal government, comes through the legal ports of entry. There could be no other way to supply the annual $150 billion demand in the United States. Roberto had an entry-level position in the industry. It was the least paid and most dangerous job. Journalist Dawn Paley lays out this system in her book *Drug War Capitalism*. Where there is a demand, there will be a supply, and where there is a supply, there will be plenty of businesses and banks ready to cash in. Major banks that have already been caught and charged for such money laundering—but never referred to as drug traffickers—include Wells Fargo, HSBC, and Citibank, to name but a few. The Chicago-based social justice collective Semillas Autónomas calls it *narco-capitalism*:

"a form of globalization in which national governments are key players in the global drug trade, and the drug trade plays a key role in expanding the control of transnational corporations over land, resources, and people. Meanwhile, these same governments adopt an official policy of 'war on drugs' as a pretext for increased militarization and for subjugating people."

I asked the geographer Reece Jones, author of *Violent Borders: Refugees and the Right to Move*, if he had ever heard an argument for closed borders that was so well-founded that it led him to question his conviction about the right of all people to have freedom of movement. He hesitated for a moment and then said no. "When I've done work on this and begun to think through what the alternative arguments are, they are pretty thin unless you are making a racist argument." Jones is also the editor of the book *Open Borders: In Defense of Free Movement*, and one of its contributing writers.

Most anti-immigrant narratives associate immigrants with negative "economic impacts, or...impacts on our cities, or crime, all of those things, they're just not true," Jones told me over the phone. "Immigrants commit fewer crimes. They benefit the economy, bring jobs, and often enhance the educational level of cities."

The negative arguments, says Jones, are false ones. "What they really boil down to are racist arguments for restricting movement and protecting some limited version of 'us' against some sort of version of a racialized other." In other words, most anti-immigration, pro-wall advocacy is driven by the legacies of white supremacy.

Indeed, upon scrutiny many justifications for hardened borders seem absurd. For example, does CBP accomplish its priority mission of stopping terrorists and weapons of mass destruction from crossing the border? There is no record of any person lugging a missile across the border while avoiding cacti and rattlesnakes in the hot sun. Nor has there been an incident, ever, of a person associated with a terrorist organization crossing into the United States through the southern border. During an interview with media, I was once asked how I would know whether a terrorist entered or not. Did I think the government would tell us? To which I responded, it's possible that a "terrorist" has crossed the border and the government has not publicly stated it. But given the way that the U.S. government fans the flames of its terror wars in places like Afghanistan, Iraq, Yemen, Somalia, and Pakistan (and equates terrorism with the Muslim religion or a person being Arab), my guess is that it would make big splash if the U.S. apprehended someone like Ayman Mohammed Rabie al-Zawahiri walking into Texas from Mexico.

Nevertheless, since 9/11 the United States has been stretching its border to approximately 100 countries on every continent via trainings and resource transfers. Washington used anti-terrorism rhetoric, for example, to justify the United States involvement with border work in Jordan. Through the U.S. government's Defense Threat Reduction Agency, a "combat support agency," Raytheon Corporation was contracted to construct a massive border surveillance system on Jordan's borders with both Syria and Iraq. U.S. Customs and Border Protection also has a national tracking center where hundreds of employees—including contractors from Deloitte, where Pivi Takala performed her art—scan every profile of every passenger headed to the United States. If anyone raises a red flag, which could mean simply having gone to Syria, then the agents can break into social media accounts, flesh out profiles, and even recommend that a person not be allowed to board a flight or be forced into secondary inspection upon arrival. U.S. agencies also use the term "domestic terrorists" to describe anti-fascist activists associated with the antifa protest network, another justification for the deployment of Border Patrol forces in Portland, Oregon, and other cities to quell Black Lives Matter protests. CBP also deployed a drone over Minneapolis to surveil demonstrations in the immediate aftermath of the George Floyd killing, and unleashed U.S. Border Patrol agents in Washington, D.C., as protests consumed the city. Other covert targets of CBP monitoring have included journalists, lawyers, and immigration rights advocates who were associated with the migrant caravans of 2018.

The criteria for who is a terrorist are broad and borderless. Yet intelligence on white supremacist groups, as revealed by DHS whistleblower Brian Murphy, has been suppressed. In a twenty-four-page complaint issued in September 2020, Murphy alleged that top DHS officials not only downplayed evidence of white supremacist violence, but also elevated examples of violence tied to left-wing groups. These allegations were corroborated by hacked communications between federal, state, and local law enforcement posted online in May 2020. An analysis of more than 300 of the documents by *The Intercept* "found repeated instances of antifa and left-wing protesting activities cast in cartoonishly grim terms alongside more substantive reports of lethal right-wing violence and threats that have received scant mention," according to journalist Ryan Devereaux. This all came home to roost, however, as the raw violence of white supremacists became the prominent national security concern following the January 6, 2021 riot incited by Donald Trump that resulted in five deaths, including Capitol Police Officer Brian Sicknick.

Is the United States Border Patrol a protectorate for a benevolent state that has only the well-being of its citizenry at the forefront? Are its agents protecting taxpayers from invading hordes of foreigners who would rob the vulnerable American public of health care, education, jobs, and affordable housing? Well, not really. In fact, it has been the U.S. government, not migrant caravans from Latin America, that has been constantly cutting Americans' access to basic services for decades in what Ruth Wilson Gilmore calls "organized abandonment." Undocumented people get counted in the U.S. Census, impact Congressional seats and the Electoral College, pay billions of dollars in taxes, but are excluded from the rights and protections granted to other taxpayers. For example, undocumented workers paid $27.2 billion in federal income taxes in 2017 (out of the $405.4 billion paid by all immigrants). Added to this are billions that go to state and local taxes. According to the Institute on Taxation and Economic Policy, undocumented workers contributed $11.7 billion in 2014, the most recent data, of which $7 billion came from sales and excise taxes. The fear that people "will take services is also not supported by the data," Reece

Jones writes, "which show that many undocumented workers pay into these programs without ever being able to access the benefits due to their status."

The oft-repeated claim that we need Border Patrol to protect U.S citizens from torrents of immigrants who have come to "steal our jobs" and drag down wages makes little sense. Such justifications omit the "race to the bottom" practices of big businesses, which attempt to maximize profit by reducing wages and benefits for their employees. In media and policy circles, all the attention goes to the migration of impoverished individuals, while the migration of U.S. corporations to foreign countries (where they pay local populations pennies for their labor and local governments little to no taxes) goes unreported. And this cross-border corporate migration has had a devastating economic impact on hundreds of communities, towns, and cities in the United States. For example, a 2018 report from the U.S. Bureau of Labor Statistics shows that since the implementation of NAFTA in 1994, U.S. manufacturing jobs have declined by 4.5 million, with 1.1 million of the loss attributed directly to the trade agreement. Also, according to the same bureau, two out of every five employees displaced from their manufacturing jobs were then hired elsewhere with a significant wage reduction. Indeed, if you correlate the 4.5 million manufacturing jobs lost between 1993 and 2017, with the 5.4 million service industry jobs gained, there is a wage reduction of $13 per hour. Not only have previous salaries been cut in half, they now come without the previous benefits. While undocumented people bear the brunt of the scapegoating for wage reductions, corporate power continues its constant breaching of borders for their bottom line, paying workers less, offer-ing few benefits, paying little or no taxes—all of which receives little scrutiny. As author Justin Akers Chacón writes, while investor classes crisscross the world with ease, borders "exist almost *exclusively* for the world's working classes, with deadly militarized borders facing the Global South."

Harsha Walia writes that these militarized lines of division cre-ate a "state-sanctioned pool of unfree, indentured laborers" whose "labor power is first captured by the border and then manipulated and exploited by the employer." It is here that we find the real bor-der, the real militarized divide between the 2,153 billionaires and the poorest 4.6 billion people.

And this is in the face of reports indicating that undocumented labor uplifts the wages of "citizen workers" (a term that should be scrutinized, given that 31 percent of the U.S. workforce consists of naturalized citizens, permanent residents, temporary residents and workers, refugees, and undocumented workers, according to Chacón). Gihoon Hong and John McLaren show that such work-ers will create as many as 1.2 million jobs by renting apartments, frequenting local businesses, and buying cars. Also, according to Douglas Holtz-Eakin, an economic adviser to both Bush adminis-trations, "Immigration is a great economic policy opportunity and it's important to document the impact of that." He was referring to a report by *ProPublica* analysts who determined that for every 1 percent in growth of immigrant population there was a 1.15 per-cent increase in the GDP. *ProPublica* claimed that if Donald Trump wanted 4 percent economic growth, as he claimed would happen under his leadership in presidential debates preceding the 2016 election, the surefire way to boost the economy would be to allow 8 million immigrants into the country.

Even economist George Borjas, an immigration restrictionist, has said that "the removal of immigration restrictions would indeed lead to huge increase in GDP: Global wealth would increase by $40 trillion—almost a 60 percent rise. Moreover, the gain would accrue each year after the restrictions were removed." If an economist often quoted by Trump and his aides is saying things like this, perhaps the time has come to reassess the world of militarized borders. Borjas has made the claim that the 1965 immigration law created the conditions to bring down wages in poorer sectors of the population, since it favored family reunification over bringing in high-skilled labor. That claim, however, has been tested and debunked by other economists such as David Card and Michael Clemens, "who have demonstrated," Reece Jones writes, "that the decline in wages identified by Borjas was due to a different sampling method that included more low-wage workers."

Does the U.S. border apparatus shield the population from crime? People who have supported Donald Trump certainly seem to think so, especially when they accept Trump's shtick that the hordes of people illicitly entering the United States are mostly dangerous MS-13 gang members, drug traffickers, and grifters who have come to leech off the system. Though I hesitate to cite studies about the demographics related to crime statistics—given the racist nature of prisons and policing to begin with—study after study has shown that undocumented neighborhoods are, in fact, among the safest in the country. One study, by sociologist Bianca E. Bersani, demonstrated that "foreign-born individuals exhibit remarkably low levels of involvement in crime across their life course," and are hence less likely to commit crimes than "native-born" populations. Another sociological study, titled "The immigration-crime relationship: Evidence across U.S. metropolitan areas," concluded that "after controlling for a host of demographic and economic characteristics, we find that immigration does not increase crime rates, and some aspects of immigration lessen crime in metropolitan areas."

In another report, sociologist Robert Adelman and criminologist Lesley Reid analyzed forty years of data in 200 randomly selected U.S. cities and concluded that immigration does not increase crime, but most likely suppresses it. Study after study after study has exposed the immigration/crime correlation as a myth, most likely a racist one, that subverts more penetrating examinations of crime and why it exists. A study by the Cato Institute found that there was a 1 in 723 million chance of a person being killed in the United States by a terrorist attack committed by a migrant. In fact, the primary terrorist violence in the United States today is white supremacist violence, as exemplified by the January 6, 2021 attack. Analyzing data gathered from 893 terrorist plots and attacks in the United States between January 1994 and May 2020, the Center for Strategic & International Studies found that right-wing attacks and plots "account for the majority of all terrorist incidents in the United States since 1994, and the total number of right-wing attacks and plots has grown significantly during the past six years. Right-wing extremists perpetrated two-thirds of the attacks and plots in the United States in 2019 and over 90 percent between January 1 and May 8, 2020."

Geographer Geoff Boyce argues that the Border Patrol should be abolished for a host of reasons. One is the Border Patrol's "ingrained culture of cruelty," he notes, citing the 2011 No More Deaths report. While media consumers in the United States have become aware of some of the egregious cases perpetrated under the Trump administration, especially forced family separations and their devastating impact on children, this sort of abuse long precedes the 45th presidency. Using 30,000 pages of records concerning children abused while in CBP custody between 2009 and 2014, the ACLU found that there has long been a pattern of intimidation, harassment, physical abuse, refusal of medical services, and deportation. Among the examples of abuse perpetrated by CBP are reports that Border Patrol agents deliberately struck a teenager with a patrol vehicle and repeatedly punched him; denied a pregnant minor medical attention when she reported pain, which preceded a stillbirth; subjected a teenage girl to a search in which they "forcefully spread her legs and touched her private parts so hard that she screamed"; and threw out a boy's birth certificate and threatened him with sexual abuse by an adult male detainee. Other reasons Boyce cites include persistent racism, exemplified by systemic racial profiling, corruption, and the "prevention through deterrence" strategy. These structural injustices form the scaffolding that keeps a deeply unjust and unsustainable system intact. "Turning a page on this era will require a decisive paradigm shift," Boyce writes. "We can begin by dismantling the Border Patrol."

When ethicist Philip Cole stood before an audience at the Conway Ethical Society in December 2012, he said, "As I see the economic, political, and philosophical arguments not working, I ask myself where the resistance to open borders comes from, and increasingly, I find myself in the world of myth and symbols." For example, immigrants are often cast as some sort of "mythic threat, like a vampire…a resource-sucking vampire." We are indoctrinated to believe that we need protection from those who want to "over-consume liberal resources and drain the liberal state of its ability to supply liberal goods." Or, he continues, we are convinced that we need to protect our sense of community and identity from those who are so different that they can't be assimilated. To crystallize the underlying sentiment in a word, Cole uses the German term *Heimat*—which could be defined as a person's deep sense of belonging and rooted fondness for a place, but simultaneously refers to a sentiment that underlies nationalism, and thus notions of national purity. Like the Trumpian slogan "Make America Great Again," *Heimat* is rooted in intolerance, fear, and a longing for an "imaginary place in an imaginary past when things were, we are told, more innocent and simple and stable. It is motion-less and changeless." According to Peter

Viereck's 1941 book *Metapolitics: The Roots of the Nazi Mind*, the determination that people were a threat to the security of the *Heimat* was a primary reason to take them to the concentration camps. In other words, they were enemies to the *Volk*, a word that has had many definitions in German, but during the Nazi era was often used to reference race, and its compound word *Herrenvolk* meant "master race." In this context, we can see that the resistance to open borders comes from a fear of the outsider—the migrant—as a contaminant of national purity and a source of unwanted change.

The "enormous symbolic power" of the border comes with a promise of maintaining an imaginary sense of stability and "unified territorial identity," says Cole. But allowing freedom of movement of all people, he argues, would challenge the world of "power, exploitation, and exclusion that have been in place since European colonialism." Open borders would help move us "toward dismantling those structures and toward building a world of freedom and equality." Perhaps in such a world Rogelio and Roberto would not have been forced into the desert, circumstances would not have driven them to risk their lives supplying people in the United States with drugs, and Brendan could have been pursuing a career other than the Border Patrol.

Building such a world, Cole said, "means imagining a radically different global order than we have now."

FOR THE CHILDREN

A MAN I had never seen before grabbed my arm. I was in the central plaza of Altar, Mexico, around dusk. It was 2004, and I was working with a delegation of students from the United States who were in Mexico to learn more about immigration and border issues. We were late for our next meeting, and I was trying to hurry the students into a van. For years I had been going to this small Sonoran town of 15,000 where thousands of people arrived every day from southern Mexico and Central America. In the central plaza—a small square filled with gazebos and benches—buses pulled up every fifteen minutes, unloading people who then gravitated to the shade of the church in what was often referred to at the time as the NAFTA exodus. The border town of Sasabe, Arizona—population 51—was but an hour's ride away on a bumpy dirt road, and vans were frequently leaving. Sasabe is a gateway into the Altar Valley, between the Baboquivari Mountains, near where I met Juan Carlos, and Las Guijas Mountains, where Roberto died in Brendan's and Rogelio's arms. This area, blazing hot in the summer and desolate, was hardly a place where people would cross before the 1990s strategy of prevention through deterrence, but now, in 2004, there was no busier crossing area.

The man, his hand still on my arm, began to talk even though I tried to indicate that I was busy. He told me his name was Alfaro. He told me that his beloved daughter—"*mi querida hija*"—had crossed the border three months earlier, and had promised him that she would call when she got to the other side. But she never did. The last

89

time Alfaro had heard from her she was in Altar, just before she left. At that point I paused and really looked at the man for the first time. The pain in his face and tenderness in his eyes I remember to this day, more than fifteen years later. Day after day after day, he waited in his home in the province of Huehuetenango, Guatemala, for his *querida hija* to call. I didn't know this man's personal history, but quickly estimated that he was most likely over fifty. There was no way he could've avoided the U.S.-trained troops marauding through Guatemala in the 1980s in a "scorched earth" campaign that left some 200,000 people dead, mostly indigenous, in what is known as the Mayan Holocaust. I also knew that Huehuetenango had some of the highest poverty rates in Guatemala—in some places above 90 percent—despite being resource rich and filled with foreign, border-breaching mining and hydroelectric dam companies. Alfaro told me he had scraped together every coin he had to travel north to this Mexican border town.

Although I was unable to help the man and never saw him again after our brief encounter, he would come back to me at certain moments. One such time was in 2016 while I was interviewed about borders by a Wisconsin radio station. During the call-in part of the show, the host patched in a caller who wanted to get something off his chest right away: He told me to stop calling "them" undocumented. He said I should call them what "they" are—"illegal." After that bit of advice, he got to the point of his phone call. How did I know that "they" were not lying? In the interview, I had mentioned the stories of different people I had met, including one of a man I met at a soup kitchen run by the Kino Border Initiative in Mexico. The man told me that he walked from Nogales to Tucson starting on December 25 and ending on January 1.

Given the dates, the man told me with a smile that this was the walk of the *Reyes Magos*—referring to the Three Kings who embarked on a trip to Bethlehem after the birth of Jesus. It was a long, bitterly cold journey along Interstate 19, the highway that goes straight north from Nogales to Tucson for about sixty miles. He had described his freezing hands and freezing feet when he was in the high canyons and mountain ranges outside Nogales, some over 8,000 feet above sea level, including the muscular Tumacacori and towering Santa Rita Mountains, also home to a wildlife corridor where a rare jaguar had been spotted that same year. His journey, he told me, was going to be his Christmas present for his son, who lived in Las Vegas. His son was about to enter college and was struggling with his finances. The man was on a pilgrimage. He was going to Las Vegas to help his son with his tuition. But when his hands and feet turned numb, and he lost direction and feared for his life, he turned himself in to the Border Patrol.

The caller insisted that the man's ordeal was *not* a "march of the Three Kings." As he ranted, I remembered all the people, over many years, who had told me that they skipped meals for their children, that they were going north to try to send back enough money so their children could stay in school, that they were going north because a child was sick, that they were going north for want of a better life for a child. Not even necessarily

91

to live in the United States, but to recapture and send back some of the wealth that had been brazenly stolen from them. In some cases, I met whole families on the move because they were concerned about the safety of their children. Almost all of the stories involved a sacrifice for a child—one generation building a bridge for another one.

For 300 years, Roman Krznaric writes, influential thinkers such as Thomas Hobbes and Sigmund Freud have been telling people that "we are essentially self-interested, self-preserving creatures who pursue our own individualistic ends," and this "dark depiction of human beings has become the prevailing view in Western culture."

As economist Richard Layard put it, however, the key to one's happiness is not self-interest, self-preservation, pursuing individualistic ends, but a "deep cultivation of the primitive instinct of empathy." "If you care more about other people relative to yourself," writes Layard, "you are more likely to be happy." Of course, the stories of border-crossers can get messy, and every context is different, but one of the prevailing dynamics is that migrations usually involve sacrifice for others. And it should be clear to even the most hardened heart that in most cases a person who leaves their ancestral home and takes enormous risks traveling to foreign soil is doing it for a cause greater than their "own individualistic ends."

According to the caller on the radio program, "they" were lying to me. It was as if he were imagining migrants doing all the things the United States and its corporate class do when they cross borders—wielding weapons and bombs and destroying communities, exploiting natural wealth, causing environmental destruction, leaving a burden on our children's children's children. Despite the xenophobia that seethed from his words and tone, the caller's narrative was an accepted discourse, and could have been expressed politely and dispassionately with a word like "destabilization." The caller's voice started to turn into white noise, and my attention drifted to the memory of Alfaro looking for his missing daughter on the Altar-Sasabe border. It was as if the vitriolic rant had summoned him. In my mind I saw the tenderness in Alfaro's eyes. And when it was finally my turn to respond, I did so by telling Alfaro's story. At the van, he had said that he was going to look for his daughter in the vast Sonoran Desert. He was going to find his daughter no matter what. As he spoke, I knew he could tear down any wall that stood between them with his bare hands.

I'll never know if Alfaro found his daughter, if he scoured the desert or was swallowed by it. But there he was, in my mind, twelve years after meeting him, when I had just become a new father myself. And he, like so many parents who have crossed the Mexico-U.S. border before him, was making a sacrifice for his child, and ultimately for future generations. And in honor of that spirit, my answer to the caller was not an angry rebuttal, nor a diplomatic acquiescence. The answer was that I, as a father, could only say that Alfaro had given me an example to live by.

TOWARD A HIGHER LAW

L.J. WAS WALKING her dogs around her house, located about ten miles from the border, when she saw five people, all dressed in camouflage, walking slowly up her driveway. At first the camo startled her, but when she approached the group she learned that they were from Guatemala, the Border Patrol was after them, and agents had "dusted" them—flying their helicopters so low that the spinning propellers threw up clouds of dust. The purpose of this Border Patrol tactic is to make people scatter, often in terror, and run for their lives. Sometimes people run over cliffs, fall into ravines, get sliced by cacti, or run into tall grass where rattlesnakes lurk. One ambulance driver described to me a situation in which a Border Patrol agent forcefully interrogated a person in the back of the vehicle. The man had run over the edge of a ravine and been severely injured. As the ambulance rumbled down the dark road toward a hospital in Tucson, the agent screamed questions at the man, who had blood gushing from his head.

The group walked slowly up L.J.'s driveway with the hardened faces of people who had been through a war, one whose consequences were almost entirely obscured from the public. She invited the group into her house. As they settled into comfortable seats, L.J. served them lots of fresh water. Everyone took showers. And while all that was happening, L.J. began to make breakfast. But it wasn't just breakfast, it was a feast, as if it were a holiday meal. She put a leaf in the dining room table and laid out cloth napkins. There were scrambled eggs (made the Guatemalan way with onions and tomatoes), black beans, corn tortillas, country fried potatoes, avocado slices, and a fruit plate piled high with melon, peaches, and cherries. "I had baked blueberry muffins the day before, and not a crumb was left," she told me.

The hardened faces softened. Soon everyone was joking and laughing, temporarily setting aside memories of thirst, hunger, the loud beating of helicopter propellers, and running away from uniformed men with guns. A friend of L.J.'s later told her, "You didn't have to do that." She said "they" were used to eating whatever canned food they could carry on their backs through the desert. They were used to drinking cloudy water, cow-trough water, bacteria-infested water.

That was the point, L.J. responded. "We need for people to feel like the human beings they are." Clean sheets, clean towels, an extravagant meal, was an appeal to everyone's humanity, including her own. L.J. knew that she was doing this at great risk, that at any given moment Border Patrol could storm her house and accuse her of numerous felonies, but when I asked her about that, she shrugged it off. She smiled and said there was nothing else she could do.

In an article comparing today's immigration laws with nineteenth-century fugitive slave laws, Manish Sinha describes an incident in the 1840s involving an elder abolitionist who was caught helping seven black people escape their white enslavers. The case against the anti-slavery activist, John Van Zandt, was litigated all the way to the U.S. Supreme Court, and the unusually harsh judgment cost him his property, sent him to jail, and caused him to be excommunicated from his church. His children were scattered across the country when he died, penniless, years later. From the time of his capture to the day of his death, Van Zandt refused to reveal the whereabouts of the people he helped liberate. As Sinha writes, the abolitionists "lost that legal battle but would eventually win the political war against Southern slavery." Their aim was to appeal to "the higher law" of humanity in their fight against white supremacy and its legal justifications for human trafficking, breeding, and enslavement of black families.

According to laws enforced by the U.S. Border Patrol, L.J.'s provision of home-baked blueberry muffins could have been a criminal act. But according to spiritual laws, religious traditions, philosophers, international law, and basic human empathy, she was doing what absolutely needed to be done. She was breaking a lower law to follow a higher one.

History is rich with similar acts, large and small. For example, the pledge of Gandhi and members of his movement in India in the 1930s: "We solemnly affirm that...we shall refuse civilly to obey these laws." They backed their words with the salt march from Ahmadabad to the beach of Dandi to cull salt from the sea in defiance of the governmental monopoly on salt and the salt tax. In his "Letter from the Birmingham City Jail," Martin Luther King Jr. wrote, "An unjust law is out of harmony with the moral law."

L.J. was also following a long, rich tradition of hospitality and humanitarian aid efforts in the Arizona borderlands, first and foremost by the Tohono O'odham long before the border even existed. However, attempts to criminalize humanitarian assistance have spanned decades, as border enforcement has ratcheted up. In 1986, the U.S. Justice Department indicted sixteen U.S. and Mexican church people on seventy-one counts of conspiracy. The charge was that these religious figures encouraged and aided "illegal aliens to enter the United States by shielding, harboring and transporting them." And more than thirty years later, No More Deaths volunteer Scott Warren faced twenty years in prison for the alleged felonies of "harboring" and "conspiracy" after Border Patrol raided a clinic where he, along with other volunteers, were assisting two Guatemalan men in need of medical aid. The group had been practicing such aid for years. Warren was unanimously acquitted by a jury in 2019. In the borderlands, humanitarian aid was also civil disobedience.

Historian Howard Zinn wrote, "Civil disobedience is inherently antinationalist because it is based on a refusal to accept the legitimacy of government as an absolute; it considers powers of government subordinate to human rights. The implication is that these rights belong to all human beings, not just those of one's own country." And thus, embedded both in the spirit of civil disobedience and the doctrine of human rights comes a supreme argument for a world without borders, an inclusive world animated by something else.

In this sense, we could take counsel from history's most famous Jewish Palestinian refugee, Jesus of Nazareth. According to Hebrews 13:2, Jesus said: "Do not neglect to show hospitality to strangers, for by so doing some people have entertained angels without knowing it." "Practice hospitality," says his apostle Paul in a letter to Romans.

Jesus was "always crossing borders," meeting with those considered outsiders, outcasts, and untouchables, and protecting them, says Pastor Alison Harrington of Southside Presbyterian Church in Tucson, Arizona. Harrington's church—the very first institution to declare itself a sanctuary for immigrants, back in the 1980s—continues to be a leading force in the resurgent movement today. For people like Rosa Robles Loreto, the church was a sanctuary in every sense of the word. She spent fifteen months living within its walls after police pulled her over for an incorrect lane change in 2014 and ICE initiated a deportation process. In a way, Pastor Harrington is embodying the Christian tradition taught through the parable of Jesus protecting a woman from stone throwers by saying, "Let the one who is without sin cast the first stone."

In my case, it would have been a felonious disregard of the "rule of law" to assist Juan Carlos by giving him a ride. But if I didn't, according to scripture, spiritual practice, and conscience, it would be a violation of a higher law. Judeo-Christian teachings have been quite clear on the matter since their first books. For example, Exodus 23:9 states: "You must not oppress foreigners. You know what it's like to be a foreigner, for you yourselves were once foreigners in the land of Egypt." And Leviticus 33–34 states that "when a foreigner resides with you in your land, you must not oppress him. You must treat the foreigner living among you as native-born and love him as yourself, for you were foreigners in the land of Egypt."

Christianity is based in Judaism, and in Judaism showing hospitality to guests is known as a "mitzvah." According to the Jewish Virtual Library, "When one knows of strangers who are hungry or need a place to relax, [hospitality] becomes a legal obligation." *A legal obligation.* The library goes on to say that some rabbis consider *hakhnasat orchim* (the "bringing in of strangers") to be part of *gemilut hasadim* (giving of loving kindness). This hospitality is embedded in the Talmud (Taanit 20b: 11–15): "Whosoever is in need let them come and eat." These words are a central part of the Haggadah, the text that sets the order of the seder, the ritual feast that begins Passover. For this reason, in April 2016, the organization Jewish Voice for Peace, in a first-ever binational seder on the U.S.-Mexico border in Nogales, "incorporated modern stories of oppression, struggle, exodus, and liberation, and created a new bilingual Haggadah that centers stories of migration struggles and cross-border solidarity."

Longtime immigration rights activist and advocate Laurie Melrood, who is Jewish and was present at the 2016 binational seder, told me in an interview that "borders have a particularly ugly and dramatic connotation" in Judaism. Melrood, whose work on border issues began decades ago when she was an active part of the sanctuary movement in Texas, said, "It is fascinating to me that the Israeli government has chosen walls as a symbol," referring to walls built around the Palestinian territories that Israel occupies, "when it was always walls that kept Jews out of the general society. Walls have also kept people from crossing into non-Jewish sections, and there were walls that surrounded the ghettos in Eastern Europe. And then to use the same symbolism is cruelly ironic." I remembered seeing portions of the concrete wall when I was in Bethlehem. With charred pillbox towers and wire-mesh sniper's nests, the walls sharply symbolized the broader world of exclusion and violence in the very birthplace of religions whose holy texts spoke of hospitality. I too felt the cruel irony.

Melrood, who has traveled to Israel-Palestine many times, has made her life a counterpoint to the notion of walls, and has long demonstrated how to move through them with skill and creativity, whether it be to prevent immigrant children from being separated from their families, or to extend radical hospitality to strangers. From the Rio Grande Valley in south Texas in the 1980s to her work in Tucson, Arizona, decades later, she has provided a safe space and sanctuary for refugees, immigrants, and modern wayfarers.

As with Judaism and Christianity, the Muslim tradition also teaches hospitality. Giving to benefit those less fortunate is one of the five pillars of Islam. "Your Lord is sure to give you so much that you will be well satisfied," says the Qu'ran (Surah Ad-Duhaa 93:5–11). "Did He not find you an orphan and shelter you? Did He not find you lost and guide you? Did He not find you in need and make you self-sufficient? So do not be harsh with the orphan and do not chide the one who asks for help; talk about the blessings of your Lord."

Indeed the "Ibn Al-Sabil," the wayfarer—a person who travels on foot, like Juan Carlos—is given much attention in the Qu'ran (Surat Al-Baqarah 2:177).

"Righteousness," says one teaching, "is [in] one who gives wealth, in spite of love for it, to relatives, orphans, the needy, the traveler, and for freeing slaves."

Like Jesus, the visionary Muslim poet Rumi was dedicated to breaking down borders and building up bridges. He taught to "ignore those that make you fearful and sad, that degrade you back toward disease and death." Rumi insisted that life is "ecstatic motion," and that the "task is not to seek for love, but merely to seek and find all the barriers within yourself that you have built against it."

The Judeo-Christian-Muslim traditions are not the only ones with such views on hospitality and the borders that prevent it. All the major religions and spiritual traditions seem to agree, including the *himdag* of the indigenous Tohono O'odham, on whose land Juan Carlos and I stood when our encounter took place.

The *himdag* refers to the beliefs, stories, and rituals that govern the relationship between a person, the larger community, and the Creator. "We are directed by Creation to maintain the area by doing our ceremonies," Tohono O'odham elder Ofelia Rivas told author Marcello DiCintio, "by doing our prayer offerings. Doing our songs to specific mountains. Gathering medicine." And because O'odham land spans from today's Mexico to today's United States, the imposed border not only "divided our territory, it desecrated it." Jaco Hamman, associate professor of religion, psychology, and culture at the Vanderbilt Divinity School and author of *Play-full Life: Slowing Down and Seeking Peace*, understands *himdag* to mean "walking in balance," and that inherent in the spiritual practice is the awakening of "hospitality."

Many Eastern practices also instruct dissolving a sense of otherness through hospitality and kindness. Buddhism, for example, clearly instructs establishing a daily practice based on loving kindness. In the Majjhima Nikāya, a collection of Buddhist discourses, one treatise, known as the Karaniya Metta Sutta, teaches, "A mother, even at the risk of her own life, protects her child, her only child. In this way, cultivate love without measure to all beings." The Buddha instructs us, "Cultivate toward the whole world—above, below, around—a heart of love unstinted, unmixed with any sense of differing or opposing interests. You should maintain this mindfulness all the time you are awake. Such a state of the heart is the best in the world." In Tibetan Buddhism, instructions are offered for training the mind in four boundless qualities—boundless love, compassion, sympathetic joy, and impartiality. In a famous teaching, Tibetan meditation master Patrul Rinpoche (1808–1887) wrote: "To make things as easy as possible to understand, we can summarize the four boundless qualities in the single phrase 'a kind heart.' Just train yourself to have a kind heart always and in all situations."

And how does all of this translate to the secular world? Author and physician Kelli Harding might have an answer. While doing research, she discovered a 1970s-era experiment using rabbits to test high cholesterol's connection with heart disease. There was one set of rabbits that, it turned out, did not exhibit the same symptoms as the others. Despite registering the same level of cholesterol, there was nothing wrong with their hearts. The curious doctors realized that the difference between the two groups was the fact that the person who administered the experiment to the healthy group of rabbits treated them with affection and kindness. She petted them, talked to them, loved them. The result was a higher level of health. This finding became the basis of Harding's 2019 book *The Rabbit Effect*. As one reviewer wrote, the book recalled Henry James's advice to do three things in life: Be kind. Be kind. And be kind.

But how can kindness translate to the social movements needed to topple the walls we see in Nogales and all over the world? Kindness might just be the foundation of what adrienne maree brown defines as emergence. "Emergence emphasizes critical connections over critical mass, building authentic relationships, listening with all the senses of the body and the mind," writes brown. "Emergent strategy is how we intentionally change in ways that grow our capacity to embody the just and liberated worlds we long for....If the goal was to increase the love, rather than winning or dominating a constant opponent, I think we could actually imagine liberation from constant oppression. We would suddenly be seeing everything we do, every-one we meet, not through the tactical eyes of war, but through eyes of love....We would organize with the perspective that there is wis-dom and experience and amazing story in the communities we love, and instead of starting up new ideas/organizations all the time, we would want to listen, support, collaborate, merge, and grow through fusion, not competition."

━

TO LEARN MORE about the notion of living by higher laws, I sought out Brother David Buer, a Franciscan Friar who resides in Elfrida, Arizona. I have known Brother David since 2011, when we walked the Migrant Trail together, a seven-day journey that spans the seventy-five miles from Sasabe to Tucson. The walk takes place every year in solidarity with people who have lost their lives and loved ones crossing the border.

Over the years I have witnessed Brother David's profound dedication to the homeless populations in Tucson and seen him spearhead projects such as the Soup Patrol in the winter and the Cooling Center in the summer. In 2012, I drove with him on a humanitarian mission run by the Samaritans, a group that searches the borderlands for people in distress and leaves gallons of water on migrant routes, among other things. It is clear to me that Brother David is an immediate example of a person living out a spiritual and higher law. But what does that mean from his perspective? And how can it be applied to people in the world who are not friars, or not even religious? How can those who view organized religion with skepticism still make use of their most vital examples in terms of living a higher law?

To find out, I took a short road trip to see him, with my four-year-old son William, in May 2020. At that moment, the pandemic was in full effect, and the Black Lives Matter movement was about to explode across the United States in response to the police killing of George Floyd. After weeks of sheltering in place, it felt great to get out of the city, into the desert, and under the big sky filled with moody clouds that hovered over jagged, muscular mountaintops. With COVID, the shutdowns, 33 million jobs lost, we were in uncharted territory—one rife with crisis but rich in possibility, the very conditions that Arundhati Roy had described. We were clearly living through a moment when things were shifting and changing and falling apart before our eyes.

During the two-hour drive, I contemplated something I had come to realize earlier: that I, too, had been seeking something spiritual, and the search had become more pronounced during the pandemic. As we drove, I kept looking over to the Chiricahua Mountains as if they were guides, the light shifting on them due to the cloudy sky, their mood both beautiful and indifferent, infused with a spirit that would persist no matter what humanity did. Since they had been around for at least 25 million years, I almost wished I could interview them, could hear their perspective on this modern era, a mere speck in their geological time. As we drove, it was impossible not to think of the border as we passed green-striped Border Patrol vehicles policing the area fifty miles away from the border. Their presence also spoke to the fact that people were likely moving through the nearby high-elevation desert and attempting to avoid surveillance, maybe under the cover of the mountains themselves. Traveling through this heavily monitored landscape, I pondered how borders expand beyond international boundaries into the nation's interior, and into our personal relationships and inner lives.

Brother David greeted us in front of his church. He wore glasses, a long gray beard, and a ripped brown cassock—probably the same one he'd been wearing when I first met him nine years earlier—and a COVID mask. We wore masks, too. Brother David's greetings were normally warm, but on this occasion they were even more so with William present. After chatting while keeping the appropriate space between us, Brother David invited me into the church sanctuary for contemplative prayer. The idea of contemplative prayer sounded refreshing and I readily agreed.

Leaving William safely outside with a video, I followed Brother David into the sanctuary. We removed our masks and sat on the wooden pews. As we sat there in silence, I looked at a statue of Saint Francis of Assisi, who was canonized two years after his death in 1228. I had long been inspired by stories of Saint Francis's love and caring for the living world around him. As I gazed at Saint Francis, two birds perched on the statue's feet, I contemplated a story that Brother David had told me about an incident that had occurred during a Samaritans' mission near Ajo, Arizona, a couple of years earlier.

It was the end of a hot day, but the sun still burned down. As Brother David hiked with six one-gallon jugs in his backpack and two in his hands, he came upon a cross, made by sticks propped up by rocks. Since they were so deep in the desert, it was an odd thing to encounter. Then he saw something next to the cross: weather-frayed clothes clinging to a human skeleton. Brother David dropped to his knees and began to pray. Then he and his group of Samaritans reported to the U.S. authorities that the remains of yet another person had been found in the desert.

Before we had entered the sanctuary, Brother David told me that the monks in his order base their lives on a Franciscan concept of overflowing love. "Not sin, not guilt, not shame," he said, "but overflowing love." This practice is perhaps best captured in Saint Francis's "Canticle of All Creatures." The canticle is a prayer to the interconnectedness between all people, animals, the living earth, God, and the broader universe—an ode to building bridges, not walls. As Franciscan friar Richard Rohr puts it, "We are made to encircle others and creation in self-giving love, generosity, blessing, and service."

I thought about what Brother David emphasized about the story in the desert: the cross, created with great care and reverence. He told me he thought it must have been made by a fellow traveler, another migrant in a similar predicament—perhaps somebody who was out of water, out of food—but who either took the time to care for another being until they passed on, or found the body and a spent a sacred moment to honor the person's death. The way that Brother David told this story was simple and direct. As I absorbed what he was saying, I was struck by a simplicity that transcended the cross and spoke to an everydayness of kind actions that seemed to embody what he meant by the Franciscan practice of overflowing love.

I began to think that the transformative power of love—whether it be inspired by the Franciscan approach, another spiritual tradition, or no spiritual tradition at all—now needed to be, at least for me personally, front and center in the push forward to another more beautiful, diverse, and balanced world, a world based in justice.

In fact, in contemporary revolutionary theory and praxis, love is an increasingly acknowledged force of social change. Argentine revolutionary Che Guevara famously said, "At the risk of seeming ridiculous, let me say that the true revolutionary is guided by a great feeling of love." An "undying love for the people" was a central guiding principle for the political organization of the Black Panther Party. "Our movement is grounded in love," says Alicia Garza, co-founder of the Black Lives Matter movement. Apache Robby Romero, while commemorating the American Indian Movement's fiftieth anniversary, wrote, "The road to freedom is a path of power. I speak not of monetary, material, or military power. I am talking about pure power, spiritual power; power to love, power to nurture, power to heal, power to endure, power to resist, power to be free."

In his often censored text *Pedagogy of the Oppressed*, Brazilian revolutionary and education theorist Paolo Freire writes: "Because love is an act of courage, not of fear, love is a commitment to others. No matter where the oppressed are found, the act of love is commitment to their cause—the cause of liberation." Moreover, writes Freire, "Only by abolishing the situation of oppression is it possible to restore the love which that situation made impossible. If I do not love the world—if I do not love life—if I do not love people—I cannot enter into dialogue."

Philosopher and radical activist Cornel West cautions that love needs to go beyond reactionary parochial borders, and explains that "love of king, love of queen, love of nation, love of race," can be "deeply reactionary forces." West says that love has to have a "universality, a scope beyond the individual—the family, the clan, the tribe, the nation." "If you're going to love," he concludes, "why not have the broadest, deepest, self-emptying kind of love that embraces everybody?"

"If love were the central practice of a new generation of organizers and spiritual leaders," writes adrienne maree brown, "it would have a massive impact on what was considered organizing." "Love is profoundly political," says feminist theorist and cultural critic bell hooks. "Our deepest revolution will come when we understand this truth."

As Brother David explained the importance of love to the Franciscan practice of everyday living, I thought of L.J.'s wonderful breakfast for the camo-clad Guatemalans, I thought of Pastor Alison Harrington opening up the Kiva of Southside Presbyterian Church to people facing deportation, I thought about Laurie Melrood's years of hospitality and service, not to the rule of law but to another, higher law. This "higher law" might have many names, only one of which is overflowing love. As I reflected on all these things in the sanctuary, I felt my own walls and barriers blowing around in the force of our prayers and meditations. At the same time, I began to hear gusts of wind whipping around outside. As I did, William walked in, wanting to know what I was doing.

When our conversation continued in the church dining hall, Brother David told me that Pope Francis—who has shown persistent concern for refugees—has spoken at length about building bridges, not walls. For example, in March 2019, while in Morocco, Pope Francis said: "Bridges are needed, and we feel pain when we see people who prefer to build walls. Why do we feel sad? Because those who build walls will end up being prisoners of the walls they build. Instead, those who build bridges will go forward. Building bridges, for me, is something that goes almost beyond human." Pope Francis then quoted the late Yugoslav novelist Ivo Andrić: "The bridge is made by God with the wings of angels....The bridge is for human communication."

The pope continued this line of advocacy in October 2020, when he issued an encyclical—the most authoritative form of papal teaching—from the tomb of Saint Francis in Assisi, Italy. Through his teaching from the saint's crypt, Francis lamented the poor cooperation among countries and warned that the forces of "myopic, extremist, resentful and aggressive nationalism are on the rise." Said the pope, "Aside from the different ways that various countries responded to the [coronavirus] crisis, their inability to work together became quite evident. For all our hyper-connectivity, we witnessed a fragmentation that made it more difficult to resolve problems that affect us all....Anyone who thinks that the only lesson to be learned was the need to improve what we were already doing, or to refine existing systems and regulations, is denying reality."

Spiritual traditions all state quite clearly that not only should people have freedom of movement, but people should always offer hospitality to others, especially if they are in need. When I talked to Poep Sa Frank Jude Boccio—a Buddhist Dharma teacher (Poep Sa) and author whose counsel I sought on spirituality, hospitality, and borders—he went further and challenged the nation-state and nationalism. I first had the idea to interview Boccio right after the publication of *Border Patrol Nation*, an examination of the massive post-9/11 expansion of the U.S. Border Patrol and its enforcement apparatus. I wanted to contrast the Buddhist teachings of loving kindness, empathy, and interconnectedness with the worldview inculcated, advertised, and put into practice by the U.S. Homeland Security regime. I suspected that Buddhist practice would indeed come across as subversive.

In 2019, I was able to sit down and talk to him about this. In Buddhism, he told me, there are "three roots of suffering"—greed, hatred, and ignorance, or delusion. "Nationalism," he said, "is an extreme form of that." It is "basically institutionalized greed. Institutionalized hatred or anger. And institutionalized delusion." You can see, hear, and feel this delusion in the media, said Boccio, you can feel the stoking of fear. As sociologist Nandita Sharma writes in the book *Open Borders: In Defense of Free Movement*, "Social formations imagined as nations have been, from the start, imagined as threatened communities, always vulnerable to destruction by various so-called foreign influences," and national-ism is "highly beneficial to the world capitalist system."

Poep Sa Boccio told me in a Tucson café that people are becom-ing displaced because of "the disparity of inequality that we see across the world which is based on greed, hatred, and ignorance or delusion." He emphasized, however, that things could change if there were a cultivation of the "understanding that we are actually in this together.

"Why can't we all understand—with climate change espe-cially—that there is not just some place where you can go? We are all in this together. Why can't we make this unified attempt to make it good for all of us? The only things that keep us from that are greed, hatred, and ignorance." This greed is perpetuated by a complex of institutions that divide people on the basis of race, class, gender. The enforcement of these divisions serves to codify forms of injustice, domination, and violence into warring cartels, corporations, and nation-states.

"This myth of separate self underlies our entire civilization," says author and philosopher Charles Eisenstein. "This dualistic view of the world pits people against each other and turns nature into something we want to control. But we can choose another story—one of interdependence and connection," a new story that Border Patrol Agent Brendan Lenihan embodied as he held hands with Rogelio, trying to save Roberto's life.

A few days after my talk with Boccio, Chicana historian and philosopher Raquel Rubio-Goldsmith approached me following a panel discussion around borders. Rubio-Goldsmith, who is now co-director of the Binational Migration Institute in the Mexican American Studies Department at the University of Arizona, was born and raised on the border in Douglas, Arizona, near Elfrida. She wondered, "Who is talking about the nation-state?"

I asked her what she meant, and she said, "It's at the root of all problems. Who is talking about that?"

Rubio-Goldsmith spoke with the incarnate wisdom of a person who has been enmeshed in a border apparatus for decades and decades, and has seen its consequences.

"There needs to be a movement," she told me, "to dismantle the nation-state."

THREE

ABOLITION

In struggling for a better world all of us are fenced in, threatened with death.

The fence is reproduced globally.

In every continent, every city, every rural area, every house.

The Power's fence of war closes in on the rebels whom humanity always thanks.

But fences are broken. In every house, in every rural area, in every city, in every state, in every country, on every continent the rebels, whom human history throws up along its entire course to assure itself of hope, struggle and the fence breaks.

The rebels search each other out.

They walk toward one another.

They find each other and together break other fences....

—The Zapatistas, Second Declaration of La Realidad,

August 1996

WHEN GIOVANNI PULLED his shoes off, his blistered feet were testimony to his journey crossing into the United States. Emergency medic Cordelia Finley immediately began to wash them. It was late July 2018. We were in Sasabe, Mexico, one half mile from the border. Altar—the town where I had met Alfaro, the man searching for his missing daughter—was sixty miles to the south of us on a rutted dirt road. Las Guijas Mountains, where Border Patrol agent Lenihan had the experience with Rogelio and Roberto, were fifteen miles away. And the location where I had met Juan Carlos was only forty miles away, but when you were walking in the heat and through the mountains, it could take days and feel like years. Giovanni's raw blisters told that story.

As we sat in the shade of a cottonwood, under a blue sky where summer storm clouds were starting to build up on the fringe of the horizon, Giovanni remained resolute. On Thursday of the week prior, Giovanni had set off with five other people into the United States during a summer heat wave on a day when the temperature hit a scalding 110 degrees. His goal was to make it to Dallas, where his brothers lived and worked.

After about a half-day of walking, his feet began to hurt. Excruciating pain followed, and persisted for the next several hours as the group walked through rocky terrain, most likely the Baboquivari Mountains. Giovanni said that the hardest part was going downhill, and he grimaced recalling it. He pointed to his shins and calves, and said there was still pain when he walked.

Giovanni's feet were deeply gashed. On the back of one foot, his skin had been rubbed away and the tender, reddish, underlying tissues exposed. One toenail had completely ripped off. After the washing, Cordelia rubbed on antibiotic cream until Giovanni's discolored feet glistened. Then she wrapped them with bandages.

Cordelia later told me later that Giovanni had something akin to "trench foot," a common ailment seen in World War I, World War II, and Vietnam. She said that such a condition was not a surprise, since this is a "low-intensity war zone, and we need to understand people's injuries in that context."

Giovanni is from a place called San Cristóbal de la Frontera on the Salvadoran border. The town is in a region that scientists have begun to call the *corredor seco*—the dry corridor—an area where droughts have risen in frequency and intensity over the last decade. He told me it hadn't rained there for more than forty days.

People's *milpas*—their plots of corn, squash, and beans—had dried out, and their crops had wilted. A 2019 report by the United Nations Food and Agriculture Organization and the World Food Programme specified that the combination of persistent, prolonged droughts and heavy rains had destroyed "more than half the maize and bean crops of the subsistence farmers along the Central American Dry Corridor," an ever expanding land mass that encompasses large parts of Guatemala, Honduras, and El Salvador. The report warned that 2.2 million people suffered crop losses and 1.4 million more were in peril. According to climate scientists doing modeling in Central America, all of this is connected to an increasingly hot planet that is damaging the web of life in ways that are difficult to predict.

As author David Wallace Wells begins his book *The Uninhabitable Earth*, climate change is "worse, much worse, than you think." For example, as I write these words in October 2020, the *New York Times* reported that "Worldwide, last month was the warmest September on record, topping a record set just a year before, European scientists announced Wednesday. It was also the hottest September on record for Europe. Northern Siberia, Western Australia, the Middle East and parts of South America similarly recorded above-average temperatures." I felt this heat palpably in Tucson where there were more 100-degree days in one year—108 of them—than ever before in its recorded meteorological history.

During that same time, plumes of smoke from hundreds of out-of-control wildfires in the United States destroyed whole towns, blotted out the daytime sun, and could be seen from space. In just

California, fires have ravaged 4.1 million acres, a land mass larger than the state of Connecticut, and destroyed 10,488 homes. And this is just a glimpse into the world embroiled in flames, as fires have also raged in the Brazilian Amazon, Australia, Indonesia, Africa, and Siberia. As climate scientist Michael Mann has explained, the heating of the Earth has caused both intense precipitation and intense drought.

On one hand, the warmer atmosphere holds more moisture and means more rain and more floods. On the other, the heating on the ground evaporates moisture and can bring ferocious dry spells, as was the case in Giovanni's community. Or in the city of Chennai, in India, with a population of more than 9 million people, which in 2019 almost lost its water supply during an extended drought.

The year 2020 brought the most aggressive storm season ever recorded in the Atlantic, with thirteen hurricanes (more than double the 1981–2010 average) surging onto shores with catastrophic wind, flooding, and deadly mudslides in Central America, the Caribbean, the Yucatán Peninsula, and the United States. This included Hurricane Isaias, which in July 2020 barreled through the Bahamas, where people's homes were still pulverized from the 2019 Hurricane Dorian, and just as the island-nation was suffering a spike of coronavirus infections. Category 5 Dorian churned over the Bahamas for almost a full day, leaving 70 percent of its largest island, with a population 50,000 people, under water. With sea level expected to rise more than six feet by 2100, such a storm surge is a hard glimpse into what's on the way.

In commercial mass media today, climate catastrophes caused by global warming don't seem to last long in the news cycle or in memory. Unless you are from the Bahamas, that is, and are among the many who tried to escape a hurricane but were denied entry to the United States because you didn't have papers. Or, as was the case in January 2021, you are a person in a caravan from Honduras facing off against the guns, billy clubs, and tear gas of U.S.-trained border guards in Guatemala and Mexico, after back-to-back hurricanes a few months earlier left you so desperate that you set off to walk thousands of miles for a minimum-wage job. The collision of the climate refugee with the border apparatus is a defining dynamic of our times and will continue to be for the foreseeable future. According to one of the world's most definitive sources of data and analysis on displacement, the Internal Displacement Monitoring Center (IDMC), there has been an average of 25.3 million people had been displaced per year since 2008 due to hurricanes, floods, earthquakes, and other sudden disasters. Climate now outnumbers war by three to one in terms of the numbers of people displaced annually. That number doesn't include what the IDMC calls slow-onset disasters from "a combination of driving factors [that] may include drought-impacts on food insecurity, or the loss of habitable land and viable livelihoods due to desertification, erosion and sea-level rise." A 2020 article from the *New York Times* titled "The Great Climate Migration Has Already Begun" estimates that as many as one in three people could be displaced across the globe by 2070, many from Central America.

As Giovanni spoke, he wove together stories of the drought: how with each step he took to escape it his pain increased, how his group had run out of food and water, and how he eventually realized he couldn't go any farther. He left the group he was traveling with, turned around, and started to walk back. For six hours he was completely lost, immersed in a high-elevation desert tangled with mesquite groves and golden grasslands but with no familiar reference points. Then he found a large puddle. He dropped to the ground and filled up a water-filtering "life straw" that he had obtained from a humanitarian aid organization. While he sat by the puddle, he took off his shoes to assess his bleeding feet. The blisters on the front of his feet had burst and the pus had dampened his socks. Trying to walk was like stepping on knives. But he moved on despite it all, until he saw the distant radio tower in Sasabe. Giovanni was lucky to get out of the desert alive.

Catastrophic climate change alone is an argument for a world without borders. The world's nation-states have failed for decades to mitigate or even adequately address the most urgent crisis to face life on Earth, while personal stories of climate upheaval like Giovanni's are compounding every day at a rate of 47 people per second. We have lived through over twenty-five years of international negotiations by governments, and each month and year registers higher temperatures and greenhouse gas emissions than the one prior. "This is the first time in human history that our planet's atmosphere has had more than 415 ppm CO_2," meteorologist Eric Holthaus tweeted on May 12, 2019. "Not just in recorded history, not since the invention of agriculture 10,000 years ago. Since before modern human beings existed millions of years ago." That level was up from 357 ppm, first measured in Hawaii's Mauna Lao Observatory in 1958. And according to a report by the Intergovernmental Panel on Climate Change, for the human world to keep global warming below 1.5 degrees Celsius, greenhouse gas emissions will have to be cut by 40 percent (to 2010 levels) by 2030, and achieve net zero by 2050. "There is no documented historic precedent," according to the Intergovernmental Panel on Climate Change, for the action needed at this moment.

Yet one palpable action that has been undertaken since 1992, when the UN first recognized climate change as a serious issue, is that the world's nation-states have built more border walls than ever before. There are currently more than seventy border walls around the world, up from fifteen when the Berlin Wall fell in 1989. Hundreds of thousands of armed border guards patrol high-tech walls, often reinforced by drones, in places such as India and Bangladesh, Turkey and Syria, Israel and Egypt. The countries fueling this mass expansion are not only fortifying their own perimeters but externalizing their borders. While the United States and European nations send training crews and equipment transfers to more than 100 countries—including India, Turkey, Egypt, Mexico, Guatemala, and the Dominican Republic—they are also historically responsible for the largest amount of greenhouse gas emissions, 27 percent and 25 percent respectively between 1850 and 2011, the World Resources Institute reports.

According to political theorist and author Benjamin Barber, the divided world needs to break the shackles of countries. In his book

Cool Cities: Urban Sovereignty and the Fix for Global Warming, Barber argues that people in cities need to claim autonomy and collaborate "with other autonomous cities, in a millennium of interdependence defined by a world without borders." Individual countries—and their "national interests," advanced by a political elite beholden to multinational corporations that sell fossil fuels—are an impediment to solving the intensifying climate crisis.

He continues: "Our sour national politics, like the stumbling nation-states that breed it, has for too long been preoccupied with ideological quarrels...that no longer capture the challenges of a post-industrial, information-based, interdependent world or address the profound threats that imperil both sustainability and justice." Not to mention countries' intrinsic exclusionary political processes where most of the world's people, like Giovanni and Juan Carlos, have no say about foreign legislation that directly affects them. Nations are not only not doing the job, says Barber, they are inherently incapable of doing what needs to be done.

Barber suggests that there needs to be a "devolution" of power to the local city level, where 80 percent of emissions come from. Cities are where most of the world's populations are concentrated. People in cities are best equipped to understand and respond to the specific regional ecological crises posed to them by a world destabilized by warming, habitat disruption, and mass extinctions. Stabilizing the climate requires a radical reconfiguring of intergovernance around the globe. Whether or not you agree with Barber's argument, it shows that while the accelerating climate catastrophe is tragic, it is also seeded with possibility.

"An abolitionist approach," writes Angela Y. Davis, "requires us to imagine a constellation of alternative strategies and institutions." Abolishing the causes of climate change, like abolishing the causes of walls and prisons, requires us to imagine beyond the language, strategies, and institutions of state-corporate indoctrination. But with climate there is a new sense of urgency, and if it remains unaddressed, people will rise up and seize the means to address it themselves.

This is exactly what happened in 2020 when, after another summer of long droughts and hot weather, farmers organized a takeover of the Boquilla Dam in the Mexican state of Chihuahua. Similar to the narrative of *Sleep Dealer*, the prescient 2008 movie that begins with a farmer in Mexico trying to break into a water well that was protected by drones, Mexico sent troops to repossess the dam and ensure that, despite a severe shortage, Mexico's water reserve would be sent to the United States to fulfill an agreement. In July 2020, the drought-stricken farmers began to earnestly protest, and by September they took the dam by force. "This is a war," said Victor Velderrain, a grower who helped lead the takeover, "to survive, to continue working, to feed my family."

"We have always dedicated ourselves to work," Velderrain told the *New York Times*, "we've never been known as protesters.

What happened at the Boquilla Dam was impressive, because we took off our farmer clothes and put on the uniform of guerrilla fighters."

RECLAIMING POLITICS OF THE MIND

"DO WILDFIRES HAVE a passport?" This is one of the questions that Louie Chaboya asks Ieva Jusionyte in her book *Threshold.* "Does the water stop at the border?" As droughts, floods, and fires become more frequent and destructive, today's disasters necessitate mutual assistance, and the border impedes such assistance for millions of people like Giovanni, Juan Carlos, and the farmers who took over the Boquilla Dam.

I met both Giovanni and Juan Carlos around the same time of year in around the same place. In both cases, the Sonoran heat was beating down upon us. And in both cases, the men had been through exceptional distress. The laws of ethical living and the spiritual traditions all obligated me to assist them. Theirs are not tales of victimhood, but rather calls to mutual assistance, a call to build bridges, or as trans liberation activist and author Dean Spade says, to making revolution together. But there is something more. I finally now see what the woman in the Nogales sanctuary meant when she asked us to "tear down the wall." We not only need to protect freedom of movement as a fundamental right, we need to change the dire conditions that drive people to migrate in the first place. We need not only to reclaim the world, but to reclaim the imagination that makes the world. I mean "we" in the border-busting sense of the word, one that draws no divisions based on race, gender, class, religion, residency status, or place of origin, a "we" that does not exclude the people that night in the sanctuary.

The interests of individual nations impede the profound global cooperation needed to solve the crises we now collectively face. Nation-states have shown what they are good at: spending on walls, on militaries, on more police, to advance the privatized economies that enrich the few to the detriment of the many. As the United States, the European Union, and Australia externalize their borders and "harmonize" their security doctrines with each other, a global separation apparatus has emerged to militarize divisions between the global North and the global South. We have reached a moment where resistance to these violent borders is not enough.

The money, organization, and coordination used for policing borders can and must be utilized to both recognize and prevent the real existential threats—climate catastrophe, runaway pandemics, and endemic inequalities. For example, wouldn't the Border Patrol's 21,000 agents better serve humanity if they were tasked to help fight global warming, rather than fighting the increasing number of people driven to our borders by its consequences? If each of those agents planted one tree a day for approximately sixty-five years, those one-half trillion trees would be able to capture 205 gigatons of carbon, reducing the carbon in the atmosphere by 25 percent, according to the article "Global tree restoration potential" by environmental scientist Jean-François Bastin et al. in the journal *Science*. Going further, the estimated cost to upgrade the United States to a fully renewable zero-carbon grid in the next ten years would be approximately $4.5 trillion, according to an analysis by Wood Mackenzie. If the U.S. eliminated CBP and ICE, (based on its 2020 annual budget of $25 billion, assuming it stayed the same for ten years), $250 billion could be redirected to building sustainable energy sources. If we eliminated DHS we'd have $880 billion to build the grid and put the brakes on global warming. It's not enough, but it is a good chunk and could bring a quarter of the country into a renewable-energy track.

The resources are already there, the money, is simply misdirected. As Marv Waterstone and Ian Shaw write in their book *Wageless Life: A Manifesto for a Future Beyond Capitalism*: "Capitalism holds over our dreams and desires a powerful source of its own self-legitimation: the ideological dyad of employment-unemployment imprisons our minds in a labyrinth of paychecks and bills. This means that the imagination is a crucial battleground for liberation….We must reclaim the politics of the mind and nourish it with fresh, liberatory resources."

I now see my hesitation in the desert before Juan Carlos as a sign that I was the one who needed help. I was the one who needed to understand the world in a new way.

A PRACTICAL, POLITICAL PROJECT

IN THE SUMMER of 1947, Sir Cyril Radcliffe was appointed to be head of the U.K.'s Boundary Commission. According to an article by

John Washington in *The Nation*, Radcliffe had two weeks to divide up the British India territories of Bengal and Punjab. After three and a half centuries, the United Kingdom was finally abdicating its colonial rule. In theory the UK was to "cede control of the crown jewel of the British Empire," as Washington put it, to its inhabitants. But it was Radcliffe—not the people from Bengal and Punjab—who would determine, in the short span of three weeks, where the borders would be drawn.

European powers, despite the appearance of decolonizing the region, merely rearranged things to exert their influence and power in new ways. As Washington writes, "What resulted was a labyrinth of confusion of over 100 enclaves (a portion of a nation entirely inside another nation), counter-enclaves (an enclave within an enclave), and even a counter-counter-enclave, in which a little pocket of India sat in a little pocket of East Pakistan which sat in a bigger pocket of India which was entirely enisled in East Pakistan." Radcliffe's partitioning was not unlike other methods in which borders have been drawn. The boundaries of the nation-states that now compose the continent of Africa were not drawn up in Kinshasa by Africans, but rather in Berlin by Europeans. This was done with no concern that doing so fractured regions united by common language, tradition, custom, and history. The boundaries created through colonial imposition remained after independence. Go to any border around the world and you will likely find that relatives, friends, and community members are on both sides of the line. This is the case among the Maasai people in southern Kenya and northern Tanzania, the Palestinian people in the occupied

territories and Israel, and the Tohono O'odham in northern Sonora and southern Arizona. These political borders, drawn in the logic of colonial domination, were designed to weaken the power of the many and strengthen the control of the few. And their militarization is a relatively recent development in human history. According to geographer Joseph Nevins in his book *Operation Gatekeeper and Beyond*, this is "highly significant" and "speaks to the extraordinary power of these lines of division and control—and the agents and institutions behind them—in shaping the very ways in which we view the world and our fellow human beings."

Borders dehumanize by blockading not only people's movement, but also the mobility of ideas, wisdom, and histories. Borders indoctrinate, exclude, and censor consciousness. Borders manipulate language and the sound of your thoughts. They organize the news and the way history is publicly taught and remembered. In this sense, their invisible power is even more far-reaching. Borders attempt to control whom you can organize with and whom you cannot, what politics you can participate in, and which ones you can't. Abolishing them is a step toward human liberation.

Harsha Walia writes, "A no borders politics is not abstract; it is grounded in the material and lived impacts of our world, scarred by warfare and warming. Like the regime of private property, borders are not simply lines marking territory; they are the product of and produce social relations that we must emancipate ourselves from."

Bridget Anderson, Nandita Sharma, and Cynthia Wright point out in the article "Why No Borders?," published in the Canadian journal *Refuge*, that "the simultaneous process of granting more freedom to capital and less to migrants is far from a contradiction and is in fact a crucial underpinning of global capitalism and the equally global system of national states." And this only reinforces the realization that the study of national borders needs to start with "the recognition that they are thoroughly ideological. While they are presented as filters, sorting people into desirable and non-desirable, skilled and unskilled, genuine and bogus, worker, wife, refugee, etc., national borders are better analyzed as molds, as attempts to create certain types of subjects and subjectivities," erasing histories, erasing struggles, erasing entire peoples. Simply crossing a border forces a person to comply with a set of power relations that reassign a person's status, a person's humanity, a person's history, a person's life, ultimately creating, fomenting, and exacerbating inequalities based on race, class, and residency status. And this is why moving toward a world of no borders is not only a "practical, political project," but an urgent one that needs the force of global social movements behind it.

UPRISING

WHEN I WENT to the Zapatista community of La Realidad in Chiapas, Mexico, in the summer of 1999, I played chess with a young man named Caralampio every afternoon, usually just as the huge storm clouds rolled in and unleashed torrential rain. I was there as part of an international peace encampment. Every morning I woke up to somebody yelling "¡*Soldados!*" When this occurred, we would run to the rutted, often muddy road that crossed through the community. You could hear the heavy rumbling of the federal military caravan long before the first armored trucks, vehicles, and jeeps invaded the autonomous indigenous community. We would stand on the edge of the road as they passed, and I would scrawl in a notebook how many vehicles, what type of vehicle, how many soldiers, what was in each vehicle (from buckets to soda cans), and what weapons they had. The soldiers were coming from Guadalupe Tepeyac, a town the Zapatistas declared as their first regional resistance center in 1994, the year of their uprising. In 1995, the Mexican military invaded the community and converted it from the Zapatista organizing hub to a heavily armed military checkpoint. When I passed through in the dead of night, the checkpoint was illuminated by a blazing bonfire whose flames cast long creepy shadows of dozens of soldiers who questioned me and the group I was with for an hour before letting us move on.

During the month I was there, my friendship with Caralampio developed through our daily chess matches that only were only half deterred by the daily downpours. It was during one of these *aguaceros* that I met Subcomandante Marcos for the first time, trotting by on his horse past where I stood under a leaky wooden shelter, his black ski mask covering his face and his emblematic pipe miraculously emitting smoke despite the rain. At the time, Marcos was truly a fugitive. Mexican President Ernesto Zedillo was after him and the rest of the Zapatista leadership, part of the reason for the daily military incursions.

Eventually I went to Caralampio's house for *pozol*—a type of corn meal that most people drank out of a plastic bottle. I followed him up a muddy trail to the *milpa* where his family grew corn and beans. We later chatted in the shade of a gigantic ceiba tree, where Caralampio told me about the difficulties of making ends meet, and how he was considering going to the United States in search of work. What did I think, he asked, of his prospects? This was five years after the United States had announced its prevention-through-deterrence strategy, five years after the wall in Nogales had been built, and five years after the implementation of NAFTA.

At the time, La Realidad had no electricity, so it was difficult to communicate with Caralampio after I left. Two years later I learned that my friend had died. Caralampio had fallen not to federal bullets, but to the long legacy of federal deprivation: chronic malnutrition. Several people had tried to get him to a regional hospital, but, according to contacts, it never happened because he was denied entry for being indigenous. Hearing the news was like eating glass. That was the moment that I committed to tear down hierarchies.

A year after I was in La Realidad, I went to another Zapatista community, Primero de Mayo, to work on a water project. It was there that I met a Tojolabal man named Severino. There were two prominent things I remember from that trip. One was that a significant part of our food supply came from the tortillas the community supplied us every day. During the month, there was a stretch of about three to four days when the tortillas significantly diminished. Nobody knew why. I had never felt so hungry in my life. I remember taking one tortilla, hot from the *comal*—a smooth, flat, round griddle—sprinkling cinnamon on it, and eating it slowly to savor every possible bite.

During that time, Severino invited me to his house, where he offered to share some *pozol*. While we both drank out of the plastic bottle, two things happened. First, he apologized for the tortilla situation. He explained that the whole community was in short supply, so everyone was cutting back. Every once in a while they had to ration. Problems, he told me, were always dealt with collectively. He apologized for the community being unable to show us more hospitality. Five hundred years of history dawned on me in that moment, a sensation that would only become more pronounced as we talked. I could only think to say that the community was showing us *more* hospitality by giving us tortillas during a shortage. I told him that where I was from, hunger was treated as an individual problem, and individuals were blamed for their own peril. I apologized for not being familiar with their collective approach.

When we finished the *pozol*, Severino brought out some pictures, including one from the Zapatista uprising. On January 1, 1994, an army of indigenous people wearing ski masks on their faces took over five major cities in Chiapas. They were demanding basic and essential rights: democracy, liberty, dignity, food, housing, health, and education. The communities' grievances went back 500 years to the European invasion and conquest. The plundering Europeans considered the indigenous people subhumans, a notion whose legacy lives on in U.S. Border Patrol culture today.

The Zapatista rebellion challenges the power structure of the nation-state and rejects its legitimacy. In an act of Manifest Dismantling, the concept discussed earlier coined by Jenny Odell, the Zapatistas never intended to take power and replicate the oppressive top-down hierarchies of nation-states, but rather organized to create a bottom-up democracy based on a thorough consultation process that involves every single person in every single community.

When Severino showed me the pictures of the Zapatista uprising, I was surprised. Until that point, I had only seen him in a button down shirt, face exposed, shoveling the cement across from me as we bantered in the hot late morning sun as beautiful blue butterflies fluttered by. In the photo, he had on a black ski mask, held an old gun, and was wearing Zapatista militant garb. "This was when we took San Cristóbal de las Casas."

"Wow," I said, "that was a momentous day, a historic day."

"It was the saddest day of my life," he responded, to my surprise.

When I asked him why, he talked about all the injustices that the indigenous communities had tried to solve without having to bear arms. He talked about the generations of indentured servitude, violence, poverty, lack of education, and malnourishment. He talked about community members walking hundreds of miles to Tuxtla Gutiérrez, the capital of Chiapas, and how the community saved every possible peso to go to Mexico City to petition for land and resolve chronic injustices.

As Trinidadian historian C.L.R. James wrote, "A revolution takes place because people are so conservative; they wait and wait and wait and try every mortal thing until they reach a stage where it is impossible to go on and then they come out into the streets, and clear up in a few years the disorder of centuries."

In 2003, the Zapatistas changed the name of their resistance centers from *aguascalientes* to *caracoles*. A *caracol* is a conch shell or snail, and the spiral of the *caracol* has deep significance in Mayan cosmovision. As the Zapatistas explain, there was an ancient appreciation for the caracol's spiral that simultaneously represents going into and coming out of the heart. The spiral is reminiscent of Paulo Freire's praxis, the circular process of transformation, composed of internal reflection with external action. In a sense the *caracol* represents the collective, the Zapatistas explain, the way words go between one person and another, and the way agreements are reached. The spiral represents the bridges that are built across time and space.

"The Zapatista revolution," writes Rebecca Solnit, "took as one of its principal symbols the snail and its spiral shell. Their revolution spirals outward and backward, away from some of the colossal mistakes of capitalism's savage alienation, industrialism's regimentation, and toward old ways and small things; it also spirals inward via new words and new thoughts. The astonishing force of the Zapatistas has come from their being deeply rooted in the ancient past—'we teach our children our language to keep alive our grandmothers' said one Zapatista woman—and prophetic of the half-born other world in which, as they say, many worlds are possible. They travel both ways on their spiral."

When the construction crews arrived in Nogales to build the border wall in 1994, it was the beginning of the most expansive phase of border militarization in U.S. history. At the same time that was happening, the Zapatistas were at the very beginning of their uprising and the launch of a global resistance movement. In many ways the Zapatistas are like Pivli Takala or Diogenes, illuminating through resistance a constellation of alternatives that has been marginalized to the fringes. While the disorder of centuries becomes more apparent through more walls, barriers, surveillance traps, prisons, and policing, the Zapatistas continue to build an autonomous alternative day by day, small thing by small thing, and do so in solidarity with other such efforts around the world. And this brings me to one of the most incredible realizations I had after that afternoon sharing *pozol* with Severino. The January 1, 1994, uprising was essential for the Zapatistas, but the soul of their resistance was a community of unreported acts of solidarity and hope, the sound of the shovel, the planting of a seed, the late-night meeting by a flickering fire, the daily act of people giving dignity to other people, including the dignity Severino gave to me as I sat in his house.

"In our dreams we have seen another world," writes Subcomandante Marcos, "an honest world, a world decidedly more fair than the one in which we now live. We saw that in this world there was no need for armies; peace, justice, and liberty were so common that no one talked about them as far-off concepts, but as things such as bread, birds, air, water, like book and voice."

"Give the Zapatistas time," writes Solnit, "to keep making their world, the one that illuminates what else our lives and societies could be. Our revolution must be as different as our temperate-zone, post-industrial society is to their subtropical agrarianism, but also guided by the slow forces of dignity, imagination, and hope, as well as the playfulness they display in their imagery and language."

The "disorder of centuries" is now upon us, and knows no borders. The solutions to our crises— driven by uprising, solidarity, imagination, and hope—will also know no borders.

"IF WE WANT TO THINK ABOUT A WORLD WITHOUT BORDERS, WE HAVE TO LIVE AS IF BORDERS CAN GO"

I FIRST LEARNED about the "disorder of centuries" quote from Ruth Wilson Gilmore, one of the most prominent modern-day abolitionists dedicated to freeing the world of prisons. Gilmore always stresses that abolition today is not just about ending incarceration, but also about "abolishing the conditions under which prisons became solutions to problems." This approach also applies to border walls: How do we shift the conditions under which borders and walls became acceptable solutions to problems? Perhaps the answer lies in not the impossible task of building a humane border, but rather the Zapatista dream of a more humane world in which concepts such as borders and prisons

139

and nation-states are seen as outmoded ways of relating to one another, like slavery.

As Angela Davis asserts, at the core of an abolitionist movement is a liberating and emancipatory politics, much like the Zapatistas', based on the truth that "things can be rearranged, reimagined, reconstructed." Abolition is not about destruction, but about restoring who we can be.

Davis asserts that the abolition movement, focused on prisons and police, also needs to take on national borders. A strong movement to abolish ICE emerged in 2018, but it needs more fuel, and it needs to challenge the border. "In the very beginning," Davis said in October 2020, "when we began to raise these issues of prison abolition" (which she traces to Thomas Mathiesen's 1974 book *The Politics of Abolition*, published in the wake of the Attica prison uprising), "people thought we were absolutely insane. How can we get rid of that which guarantees safety and security to the entire population? Of course, now we are at a different point. And this would not have occurred without the activism, the intellectual labor, the organizing, the artistic labor. I think that it's important now to think more capaciously about the meaning of the nation-state and recognize that these borders will not be with us forever."

Indeed, Davis continued, the United States "has not been called the United States for very long," and given the devastating impact of settler-colonialism on indigenous nations, "the first people of this country should cause us to focus less myopically on the meaning of the United States of America." Angela Davis advocates that people use abolitionist strategies to "engage in a process of imagining what a world would look like without borders."

But what does this mean on the ground? How can this be a practical political project?

During an April 2020 presentation, Gilmore listed how many people and institutions are part of the contemporary abolitionist project, some without even knowing it: faith organizations, neighborhood organizations, artist organizations, tenant organizations, prisoner organizations, libraries, environmental justice, legal aid, transit workers, rights advocates, public health advocates, bail funds. Gilmore detailed the broad number of people coming together to try to "relieve the stress of organized abandonment," the term she uses for neoliberal austerity measures.

Indeed, like prison abolitionists, resisting this organized abandonment was partly what propelled Severino and the Zapatistas to rise up on January 1, 1994. The states of Mexico, Canada, and the United States on that day had implemented the North American Free Trade Agreement opening the borders to corporate power, while militarizing the border for everyone else. The organized abandonment of ordinary people in Mexico had begun over ten years prior with the IMF restructuring of its economy, eliminating subsidies and other benefits to small farmers and the working class. But the migration following NAFTA may have exceeded the suppositions of U.S. officials, even INS commissioner Doris Meissner, who correctly predicted massive displacements in Mexico. The nation-state solution was to fortify the border, build hundreds of prisons to incarcerate people without status, and enact the deterrence strategy that would be the very reason that I came face to face with Juan Carlos in the middle of the desert on that hot September day. The nation-state solution to organized abandonment was to enact a militarized system of exclusion. It didn't matter what precise version of organized abandonment displaced Juan Carlos—maybe it was climate change or economic dispossession or both, maybe he was facing the bullets of armies or police or gangs—the desert where he could die was the "solution."

In this sense, for an abolitionist solution to today's border issues, we need to look no further than the indigenous rebel communities in Chiapas as an example. The Zapatistas didn't slowly come around to the NAFTA issue and how it allowed people in Mexico to be exploited by large foreign corporations, undermining small farmers, threatening protected communal land with privatization and the theft of natural resources. All of this was addressed when Severino stood in San Cristóbal and the Zapatistas called NAFTA "a death sentence to the indigenous people."

Instead of spending billions on walls and the militarization of the border, if immigration restrictionists were serious about a solution—and this includes liberals who have opined that border enforcement is practical, and that anything less would invite instability—they would be thinking more about supporting movements to improve access to clean water, education, and health care and to end chronic poverty, the very goals of the Zapatistas and many movements around the world. The militarized border serves to manage the instability and ensure that the business as usual of "organized abandonment"—the extracting, polluting, or compromising the very resources that people need to survive and live with dignity—continues unabated. Rather than alleviate destabilization, by enforcing segregation the world's borders keep it intact.

According to statistics from the United Nation's Food and Agriculture Organization, there are 815 million people (twice the population of the United States) who do not have enough calories to sustain "minimal" human activity, and 1.5 billion who are food insecure, meaning without enough calories to sustain "normal" activity. All together, 2.1 billion people on planet earth suffer from malnutrition.

The internationally agreed upon poverty line of $1.90 per day used by the United Nations to claim that "global poverty rates have been cut by more than half since 2000" remains highly contested by economists and scholars such as David Woodward. According to Woodward, this would be like thirty-five people trying to survive in Britain "on a single minimum wage, with no benefits of any kind, no gifts, borrowing, scavenging, begging or savings to draw on (since these are all included as 'income' in poverty calculations)."

Economist Jason Hickel explains that 4.2 billion people currently earn $7.40 per day or less, six times more than in 1981. Even that divide would not include *maquila* workers in Nogales, Mexico, who currently earn $8 a day working in windowless factories making cotton swabs, bank pens, suitcases, locks, and electronic components for aviation and surveillance. A half-day's wages is enough for a worker to buy a carton of milk and a dozen eggs. Today, under-ventilated *maquilas* expose workers not only to hazardous vapors, but also to increased risk of exposure to COVID infection. A June 2020 study reported that young people in Mexican border cities like Tijuana who had jobs or ties to *maquiladoras* were dying from the coronavirus at a rate twenty-five times higher than the same demographic just north of the border.

Hickel says that establishing a poverty line at $2 a day is "an insult to humanity." What should be loud and clear is something else, what Oxfam International stated in a headline in January 2018: "Richest 1 percent bagged 82 percent of wealth created last year, poorest half of humanity got nothing."

Indeed, "border security" takes on a whole different meaning when framed as an apparatus to enforce extreme inequalities and power imbalances. It is not a protectorate of the people, a solution to a problem, but a system where the rich get richer, the poor get poorer, and the planet remains "stable" for the rich and powerful as the ecosystem heats up and destabilizes. The solutions become much different when we reframe "immigration reform" honestly. And the Zapatista response becomes a solution. The Zapatistas' international movement to create "one world in which many worlds fit" commits crimes against injustice, and this fugitive process creates Akomolafe's sanctuary where new worlds are waiting to be born, spaces that divest from the old ways of organized abandonment and invite new connections based on our common humanity and interbeing with the natural world. "We do need to get back on the streets," write the Zapatistas in October 2020. "As we've said before, life, and the struggle for life, is not an individual issue, but a collective one. Now we see that it's not a national issue either, but a global one."

According to Gilmore, anything a person does to alleviate the root conditions of injustice helps the project of abolition and helps tear down the wall, the prison, the nation-state. Sure, we could take chain saws to the wall and risk getting shot by the border patrol, but abolition doesn't have to involve lethal risk. Instead, it aims to awaken people's deepest sense of humanity by drawing on our potential to be creative, collaborative, and inclusive. Our efforts to organize, resist, and create alternative institutions can involve a process of what Gilmore calls "non-reformist reforms"—steps that bring us closer to our goals without reinforcing the hierarchies of injustice.

For example, if comprehensive immigration reform proposes $45 billion toward border militarization, as did the proposed bill in 2013, or claims that it will "fix" a broken system, then it reinforces an expanding massive complex and sustains an authoritarian society. On the other hand, examples of non-reformist reforms would include the Deferred Action for Childhood Arrivals (DACA) program, legalization of driver's licenses for people without residency status, and ending police/DHS collaboration, since such changes come into being through organizing social movements and do not contribute additional resources to the enforcement apparatus. In this sense, as the administration of Joe Biden and Kamala Harris make public reversals of Trump-era border and immigration policies, it is important to stop them from fortifying the border apparatus in other ways. Indeed, there might not be a more optimal time to push for non-reformist reforms, but it will take diligence and an understanding that historically Democrats—such as Bill Clinton and Barack Obama—have been complicit in expanding the apparatus. The border immigration system is bipartisan, and abolition has to depart from partisan thinking.

Non-reformist reforms could also mean anything that diverts money away from hierarchies of injustice, like defunding police at home, defunding border enforcement at our perimeter, and defunding U.S. occupations of Iraq and Afghanistan abroad. Doing so would free up billions of dollars that could be used for education, health care, housing, and developing a renewable energy grid that frees us from the fossil fuels contributing to global warming. The long arc of abolition does not have to be abstract; it can be constructed in the small steps, based on direct community needs, of a practical political project.

And, as Gilmore says, the key is presence. "If we want to think about a world after borders," Gilmore said, "then we have to live as if borders can go."

"WHAT IS IT GOING TO TAKE?"

WHEN JACQUELINE ARELLANO stepped up to the mic in Tucson's Kennedy Park in early June 2019, she took the proverbial gloves off. She had just completed the seventy-five-mile Migrant Trail Walk from the border to Tucson—the same walk where I had met Brother David. Arellano said she lived on the border, near San Diego, and for many years she had anesthetized herself in response to the constant violence and pain. Now, she was a part of the Border Angels solidarity organization that leaves water in the desert for clandestine border crossers like Juan Carlos. Arellano's voice was simultaneously raw, exasperated, and tender as she said: *What is it going to take? What is going to take gather people into a critical mass that will bring this border down?*

As she spoke, I remembered how it felt at the end of the seven-day walk. I had done it four times myself, but this time I just came to greet the walkers as they finished, and had brought William, then three years old. Even if you are in no way trying to mimic what people have to do crossing the border—even with access to water and food—the walk is difficult. At one point, it's as if the singular person ceases to exist and you exist, as part of a group with a common goal to walk seventy-five miles through the blazing hot Arizona desert. As the miles increase, everyone begins to feel injured and increasingly uncomfortable. Eventually, each step becomes a prayer, and the space the group inhabits feels like a moving sanctuary. By the end of the those seventy-five miles, the feeling is that maybe we could do something spectacular, perhaps the normal paradigm could change, can change, is changing, we can mold it into something else with only our bare hands, hearts, and grit. But it's more than that, as Arellano's soaring voice said, *Things have to change*. There is no way we can permit things to stay the same. "We're going to crush the wall," William said, catching the drift of Arellano's speech, and giving it again the child's understanding that things can be rearranged, reimagined, and reconstructed. "And then we are going to turn it into bikes."

On the eve of the last day of the Migrant Trail, before arriving at Kennedy Park in Tucson, walkers camp at a place that organizers have affectionately called "Hell Camp" since the first walk in 2004. During the day there is no shade, temperatures often exceed 100 degrees, and the ground sparkles with shards of glass baking in the June sun. In the morning, up on a canyon ledge, there is a closing ceremony for the walk. At this point, there are just seven miles to go. From the ledge you can see where you have walked—the Baboquivari Mountains, the deserts around Three Points, the Altar Valley all the way to the border at Sasabe. As the sun rises over the ceremony, you can see the vast expanse of borderlands, the mountains like distant waves, the colors orange and tender as if they, too, spoke a new language, if we could only listen. With the view comes a grounded knowledge that there are people we cannot see in the distance, but they are out there walking, enduring, with no food, no water, no backup cars to support them. I can see the place where Brendan helped Rogelio, I can see the place where Giovanni was lost, I can see the place where I stood looking at Juan Carlos with hesitation. It is the place where Alfaro found himself searching for his missing daughter. There is nothing like looking over that land mass and knowing in your bones and blood and brain that you can no longer ignore life's interconnectedness, that you have irrevocably changed. The view is so vast from the ridge that you can see things beyond the limit of one lifetime, you can glimpse geological history that spans billions of years. There is a profound affinity, not with a country, but with the land, humanity, the living Earth, and the web of life.

A day after taking in the view and completing her seventy-fifth mile of the walk, Jacqueline Arellano asked out loud what it will take to break this thing, the border, and the wall of polices that enforces it. One year earlier, in 2018, Arellano had hoped that the outcry against family separation might finally do it. But no, she says, oppression "just becomes normalized."

What is it going to take?

As Arellano spoke, I was amazed at the absence of media, with just the majestic silence of the rolling Tucson Mountains behind us. But Arellano and her group of walkers didn't seem to care if media were there or not. They had just spent days purposely disconnected from the world of news, media, and internet so as to more fully engage with the vast open spaces people struggle through to escape the death sentence of corporate migration, impoverishment, perse-cution, and organized abandonment. Having completed their jour-ney, the walkers were people transformed. Because when you finish the seventy-five miles together, you feel like you could walk another seventy-five miles again back to the border wall and tear it down, maybe with your bare hands, or maybe with words and stories and voices and tears and a thousand unanswered questions like: *Have you seen my daughter? Can you give me a ride?*

What if hundreds, thousands, millions of people—from the south and the north--gathered together at borders around the world to say, like the Zapatistas, *¡ya basta!*—enough is enough. What if the power of our children's sweet voices were joined by the force of our ancestors? In Arellano's voice and presence I could feel the tremors that might crumble nation-states and reveal the shape of the bridges that have been waiting to be built for so long.

That's what it felt like when Arellano asked again: *What is it going to take?*

A revolution. Arellano says it's going to take *a revolution.*

A SPACE WHERE EVERYONE IS

IN THE FINAL chapter of her book *Are Prisons Obsolete?*, Angela Davis writes about a young white student named Amy Biehl who was driving some black friends to their home in Guguletu, South Africa. It was 1993, three years after Nelson Mandela was released from prison, but before he became president. Biehl was on a Fulbright scholarship, studying women's roles in the creation of a new constitution for the post-apartheid society. During the drive, a crowd emerged from an anti-apartheid rally shouting anti-white slogans and ambushed Biehl in her car, killing her. Four men were arrested,

150

tried, convicted, and sentenced to eighteen years of prison. Amy's parent's, Linda and Peter Biehl, however, decided to support the amnesty petition of the four men as put forth by the South African Truth and Reconciliation Commission. At the amnesty hearing, the Biehls shook hands with the families of the perpetrators. To explain their presence, Peter Biehl quoted from Amy's own previous writing about building bridges in the aftermath of apartheid: "We are here to reconcile a human life which was taken without an opportunity for dialogue. When we are finished with this process we must move forward with linked arms."

As Davis reports, two of the men convicted, Easy Nofemela and Ntobeko Peni, later met with the Biehls. Nofemela expressed his own sorrow about killing their daughter and said, "I know you lost a person you love. I want you to forgive me and take me as your child." Since then Nofemela and Peni have been working for the Amy Biehl Foundation Trust in Cape Town, founded to develop and empower youths in the townships and to discourage further violence. Linda Biehl said, "It's what Desmond Tutu calls *ubuntu*: to choose to forgive rather than demand retribution, a belief that 'my humanity is inextricably caught up in yours.'" Tutu maintained that, through *ubuntu*, South Africans were able to deal with apartheid-era political crimes by seeking restorative justice rather than retribution against their oppressors.

As Jacqueline Arellano stood at Kennedy Park and said, "It is going to take a revolution," the spirit of how that might look can be seen in the Biehls' story and the South African (specifically, Nguni) practice of *ubuntu*. Can we transform our language, relationships, and institutions in ways that do not re-create hierarchies of domination, but rather facilitate emancipatory values that allow humanity, as a whole, to restore itself and the living world? Can we, while seeking to liberate ourselves from oppression and division, also include those who have oppressed and divided us? In such a situation Joanna Macy, for one, asks for a transformative empathy: "When you bump up against people who are working for the system in corporations or government or military or police or Monsanto or what have you, you realize that they are not the enemy, that they are just in bondage to these organized forms of greed, hatred, and delusion."

Which brings us to the question: If we can build these kinds of bridges, can we, as Paolo Freire holds, actually create a world where it's *easier to love*?

These are big questions, but they are the questions of our time time that beckon our attention. "To affirm that men and women are persons," writes Freire "and as persons should be free, and yet do nothing tangible to make this affirmation a reality, is a farce."

The modern-day abolition movement asks us to reject the farce of doing nothing tangible to affirm our freedom. In this rejection, 1,000 other previously unexamined alternatives emerge. These alternative ways are based on new social dynamics that elevate openness and humanity over domination and division. This includes restoration and inclusion over punishment and control. And it includes creative coalition building and collaboration, even among unlikely allies.

In their article in *Radical History Review*, "Joining Forces: Prisons and Environmental Justice in Recent California Organizing," Rose Braz and Craig Gilmore describe how politically divergent organizations such as the Friends of the Kangaroo Rats, the Madres de Este LA, and abolitionist groups came together to successfully stop another prison from being built in California's San Joaquin Valley. Through organizing and solidarity, these groups converted their differences into a formidable source of politically diverse power. As sociologist and longtime abolitionist Zoe Hammer explained to me, this "is very against the 'woke' common sense of how we organize, it's not about having the same exact politics." As Hammer has been telling her students for many years, "If you are going to write something about what we can't do, what we can't say, or who can't play, I don't want to hear it....Because I'm going to give it back to you and ask you what we can do, what we can say, and who can play. And that comes out of my experience in abolition organizing."

A movement gains strength as we tear down the walls within ourselves, as did the Biehls, and between ourselves and others, no matter our differences. It is a space of inclusion that rejects the dogmatic polity of purity—the "us versus them"—whether it comes from a nation-state and its borders or from the divisions within our own social movements. Ultimately, it is the power of transformative relationships that allows us to cross bridges and enter the portal that Arundhati Roy describes in words that bear repeating: "We can choose to walk through it, dragging the carcasses of our prejudice and hatred, our avarice, our data banks and dead ideas, our dead rivers and smoky skies behind us. Or we can walk through lightly, with little luggage, ready to imagine another world. And ready to fight for it."

And "this fight," writes Freire, "will actually constitute an act of love opposing the lovelessness that lies at the heart of the oppressors' violence." To muster such forces and sustain them is, in Brother David's Franciscan language, to practice overflowing love. When I was in La Realidad in August 1999, the Zapatistas described this process as "planting the trees of tomorrow."

"In that tree of tomorrow is a space where everyone is, where the other knows and respects the other others, and where the false light loses its last battle," said Subcomandante Marcos. "If I were pressed to be precise, I would tell you that it is a place with democracy, liberty and justice: That is the tree of tomorrow."

To plant such a seed, I tear down the wall within myself, between you and me, between us and them.

I am back in the desert face to face with Juan Carlos, but I'm the one who is disoriented. Suddenly the desert, Juan Carlos, and I are one thing. I feel a deep thirst I've never felt before, Juan Carlos gives me water that I drink down in one fierce swig. I feel lost and ragged and look at the vast desert all around me, but then the Baboquivari Peak, the dirt road, the beautiful twisting saguaro, prickly pear, and cholla cacti begin to orient me. There is a world of immense beauty and love for all living beings, they say, and it is right here, in this very place, in this very moment, all you have to do is move toward it. I look at Juan Carlos. *Can you help me get there?* From him, unlike me, there is no hesitation at all. And we begin to walk together to that place where everyone is.

ACKNOWLEDGMENTS

FIRST AND FOREMOST I want to thank Greg Ruggiero for his brilliant ideas, masterful editing, eternal patience, and lovely friendship. Gracias, compa.

There are many people whose ideas are infused in the prose either via conversations, writings, both of the above, or just watching their actions in the world. Here is a partial list of those who I owe much gratitude: Alex Sager, Reece Jones, Guadalupe Castillo, Raquel Rubio-Goldsmith, Chrysta Faye, Brendan Lenihan, Joseph Nevins, Bayo Akomolafe, Michael Marder, Nandita Sharma, Ruthie Wilson Gilmore, Angela Davis, Zoe Hammer, John Gibler, Marvin Waterstone, Frank Jude Boccio, Roman Kznaric, Alison Harrington, Laurie Melrood, Blake Gentry, Dora Rodriguez, John Washington, David Garcia, Larry

Gatti, Keith Zabik, Jenny Odell, Geoff Boyce, Brother David Buer, Jacqueline Arellano and the Migrant Trail Walk, and the Zapatistas, especially Severino and Caralampio, RIP.

A special thanks to the People's Defense Initiative for attempting to make the city of Tucson a sanctuary, many words in this book have been inspired by your efforts. And No More Deaths, Samaritans, and Humane Borders, through you I have learned about radical hospitality and living as if borders could go. I want to thank the fine people at City Lights Books who brought this book to life: Elaine Katzenberger, Chris Carosi, Stacey Lewis, Gerilyn Attebery, and the great Lawrence Ferlinghetti. Thank you, Elizabeth Bell, the book became better for your edits. Thank you, Kevin Caplicki, and everyone at Just Seeds. Thank you to the visual artists whose work appears within: Carol M. Highsmith, Chip Thomas, Rochelle Brown, Dan Meyers, Andreea Popa, and the Zapatista muralists of Oventic, Chiapas, Mexico.

Thank you Peggy and Dennis for putting up with me as I wrote chunks of this in Oregon. Also thanks to Tom and Shannon, Kim and Wes. Always eternal gratitude to Mom and Dad, and my brother Mark.

Memito and Sofia, this book is for you and the children that come after you. You are the inspiration behind every word I write. As are you, Lauren. I can't tell you how grateful I am for the support and inspiration you've given me for so many years.

You have long been on the front lines showing that creating a better world is not only possible, it's possible right now. If only I could come remotely close to living up to your example. As go the words in Mary Oliver's poem, "The Greatest Gift": *"I find my soul clapping its hands for yours more than my own."* I love you.

ABOUT TODD MILLER

TODD MILLER HAS researched and written about border issues for twenty years, the last ten as an independent journalist and writer. He resides in Tucson, Arizona, but also has spent many years living and working in Oaxaca, Mexico. His work has appeared in the *New York Times*, the *San Francisco Chronicle*, *TomDispatch*, *The Nation*, *The Guardian*, *Guernica*, and *Al Jazeera English*, among other places. Miller is the author of three books: *Empire of Borders: The Expansion of the U.S. Border Around the World* (Verso, 2019), *Border Patrol Nation: Dispatches from the Front Lines of Homeland Security* (City Lights, 2014), and *Storming the Wall: Climate Change, Migration, and Homeland Security* (City Lights, 2017), which was awarded the 2018 Izzy Award for Excellence in Independent Journalism. He's a contributing editor on border and immigration issues for *NACLA Report on the Americas*.

Have Black Lives Ever Mattered?
By Mumia Abu-Jamal

Dying to Live
A Story of U.S. Immigration in an Age of Global Apartheid
By Joseph Nevins, Photography by Mizue Aizeki

Narrative of the Life of Frederick Douglass, an American Slave,
Written by Himself
A New Critical Edition by Angela Y. Davis

CITY LIGHTS BOOKS | OPEN MEDIA SERIES
Arm Yourself With Information

9 780872 868342